Mental Resilience

Build Unshakable Confidence and Stop Negative Thinking in 30 Days with Simple Daily Practices

Sage Lifestyle Press

© Copyright Sage Lifestyle Press, 2025 - All rights reserved.

The content within this book may not be reproduced, duplicated or transmitted without direct written permission from the author or the publisher.

Under no circumstances will any blame or legal responsibility be held against the publisher, or author, for any damages, reparation, or monetary loss due to the information contained within this book. Either directly or indirectly. You are responsible for your own choices, actions, and results.

Legal Notice:

This book is copyright protected. This book is only for personal use. You cannot amend, distribute, sell, use, quote or paraphrase any part, of the content within this book, without the consent of the author or publisher.

Disclaimer Notice:

Please note the information contained within this document is for educational and entertainment purposes only. All effort has been expended to present accurate, up-to-date, and reliable, complete information. No warranties of any kind are declared or implied. Readers acknowledge that the author is not engaging in the rendering of legal, financial, medical or professional advice. The content within this book has been derived from various sources. Please consult a licensed professional before attempting any techniques outlined in this book.

By reading this document, the reader agrees that under no circumstances is the author responsible for any losses, direct or indirect, which are incurred as a result of the use of the information contained within this document, including, but not limited to, — errors, omissions, or inaccuracies.

Contents

Free Bonus — IV

Introduction — V

1. Understanding the Roots of Mental Resilience — 1
2. Cognitive Behavioral Strategies — 13
3. Building Emotional Resilience — 26
4. Overcoming Self-Doubt and Inner Criticism — 41
5. Understanding Anxiety Triggers — 57
6. The Power of Positive Psychology — 73
7. Mindfulness and Meditation Techniques — 87
8. Social Connections and Support Systems — 105
9. Empowerment Through Action — 117
10. Creating Your Foundation for Long-Term Success — 132

Conclusion — 137

30-Day Transformation Plan — 139

References — 144

The Self-Love Challenge

30 Days To A More Confident you

Free Download to Walk You True a Truly Transformational Month. Giving You the Tools You Need for Daily Well-Being,

Introduction

Carmen is visiting her grandmother, who has dementia, at an old age care facility. Her grandmother has always been a storyteller at heart, and this time, she's talking about negative people, but she's not referring to them as negative people per se; she calls them Porcupines. These individuals have developed a defensive and sharp demeanor, similar to the quills of a porcupine, because of life's experiences. They are not inherently negative, but their fear and pain have shaped them into defensive beings.

We are all prone to jumping to the worst-case scenario, overthink, and lean into it because it feels much safer, too. The mind runs these patterns in the dark hours before dawn, during crucial meetings, and in daily decisions. This automatic tendency to focus on potential problems becomes our default mindset. But here in the care facility, a grandmother with a lifetime of observing human nature offers a simpler way to understand these patterns.

The late afternoon sun casts long shadows through the window as her grandmother straightens in her chair. She worked at the municipal office for thirty years, watching people come and go with their problems, worries, and complaints. She saw how negativity spread through families, offices, and entire neighborhoods. But amidst this, she also witnessed something remarkable—how some people seemed immune to it all, moved through difficulty with grace. It was as if they influenced the surrounding energy without saying a word.

Her wisdom, gained from a lifetime of observation, is a beacon of light in the darkness of negative thinking, offering us a profound understanding.

Her hands, now spotted with age but still steady, smooth the blanket across her lap. "People think negative people are the problem," she says. "But that's not true. They're just scared, scared in a way that makes them sharp, like porcupines. Nobody is born this way. Life shapes them, one small hurt at a time, until their quills grow long and strong." She pauses, looking out at the garden where other residents stroll between the flower beds. "But once you understand them, like really understand them, everything changes."

Negative thinking patterns reshape the brain's neural pathways and create deep grooves of habit that seem impossible to escape. However, ancient wisdom and modern science show that we can rewire these patterns. This demands courage, yet it's within your reach. Not through force or resistance, but through understanding and seeing what lies beneath the surface, you can take control of your thoughts and reshape your mind and build mental resilience.

Chapter One

Understanding the Roots of Mental Resilience

Building mental resilience starts with understanding what breaks it down. When we learn to recognize the patterns that undermine our mental strength, we can rebuild it stronger than before. This chapter explores how negative thinking develops and, more importantly, how understanding these patterns becomes the foundation for unshakeable mental resilience.

Rain streaks the room windows. In the back row of a workshop sits a man whose phone screen flashes every few minutes, his leg bobbing continuously under the table. When the group facilitator asks him to introduce himself, he stares into his coffee cup and mutters that his team leader thinks he needs to work on his mindset.

But his restless movements tell a deeper story: this is how the brain operates when it has learned to expect the worst at every turn. Simple patterns and experiences steadily build negative thinking, forming mental habits based on what we've learned through time. Pessimism takes root through challenging work experiences and daily setbacks, stacking up methodically until they create automatic responses that feel like protection but limit our view of what's possible.

This protective instinct shows up everywhere. A mother reading a text from her daughter missing dinner might assume she's at fault. A talented amateur musician avoids open mic nights, believing that one past mistake from three years ago defines his skills. These are just a few examples of how our minds can create negative narratives based on experiences.

Behind these patterns lies a mind hyper-focused on rejection, failure, and judgment. To change these patterns, we must teach ourselves to see them without criticism or to dig through old wounds. We must recognize how the mind learns about its defensive habits and why they once kept us safe. This recognition is the first step towards change, and it unlocks our potential for growth and transformation. Understanding these patterns is how we build true mental resilience—the ability to bounce back stronger from whatever life throws our way.

The Neuroscience of Negative Thoughts

The brain processes two hundred negative experiences more strongly than one thousand positive ones Acevedo et al. (2014). This explains why we remember the critical comment in a performance review while forgetting pages of praise, or why a single social mishap can overshadow dozens of successful interactions. Our brains have developed this way for a good reason—throughout human evolution, missing a single danger could prove fatal, while missing a single opportunity rarely had such dire consequences.

Modern neuroscience reveals how this ancient programming continues to shape our daily thought patterns. When negative thoughts activate the amygdala, a small almond-shaped structure deep in the brain, it triggers a cascade of stress hormones that put us on high alert. The prefrontal cortex, responsible for rational thinking and planning, becomes less active while the threat-detection circuits take over. This switch in the brain from the prefrontal cortex to the amygdala highlights how even clear thinkers can be overwhelmed by worst-case scenarios when faced with stress. Understanding this can empower us to manage our responses and regain perspective under challenging situations.

> This negativity bias, while once protective, can now undermine our mental resilience if left unchecked.

Brain imaging studies show that negative thoughts create stronger neural pathways with each use, similar to how a path through a field becomes more defined as people walk on it. When someone worries about an upcoming presentation, rehearses past mistakes, or imagines future failures, they strengthen these neural pathways. The brain becomes increasingly efficient at producing these thought patterns, making them feel automatic and valid even when evidence suggests otherwise.

Yet this same neuroplasticity that reinforces negative thinking also offers a way forward. The brain continues to form new neural connections throughout life, responding to new experiences and learned behaviors. This is the biological foundation of mental resilience—our capacity to literally rewire our brains for greater strength and adaptability. Understanding this biological foundation helps explain why negative thinking can feel so automatic and why targeted practice can create lasting change Acevedo et al. (2014).

Identifying Your Triggers

Our triggers reflect our unacknowledged needs, particularly where we feel most vulnerable—where time collapses between the past and the present. A simple " urgent " email catapults us to every moment we've felt overwhelmed and unprepared. A pause in conversation brings back the childhood memory of standing alone at recess. The body remembers these moments before the mind can rationalize them away, turning mundane interactions into minefields of emotional response.

Consider how a theater stage works—when a spotlight hits the correct mark, it illuminates everything in its path with stark clarity. Our triggers work the same way, throwing light in the exact places where we've learned to expect pain. The colleague who never quite looks us in the eye triggers the fear of being overlooked. The phone call we hesitate to make reveals our deep-seated fear of confrontation. These aren't random reactions—they're precise coordinates on the map of our unmet needs, pointing directly to where we've learned to armor ourselves against life.

The Five Root Causes of Negative Thinking

Lydia is sitting right across from her therapist. "We've talked about this, Lydia," she says. "You've been performing at the top of your department for three years. Every evaluation confirms this, but you still tell me you're not good enough for the promotion." Lydia stares at her hands; the bitten-down nails reveal more than her words. "I know what the evaluations say," she whispers, "but what if they're wrong? What if everyone finds out I've been lucky all this time?"

Negative thinking rarely emerges from a single source; it is an interplay of different factors that shape how we process our experiences and interpret the world. Years of research and clinical observation highlight five primary drivers: lack of confidence, perfectionism tendencies, stress and anxiety, trauma, and experiences. These factors often work together and reinforce each other in ways that can make negative thinking feel inevitable.

Let's analyze each factor's origin.

Perfectionism

We often mistake perfectionism for high standards. A perfectionist carries an internal rulebook filled with impossibly high standards. They usually turn everyday tasks into sources of intense pressure. Overworking on minor details causes missed deadlines and self-criticism.

The negative thinking comes from the gap between these impossibly high standards and the usual imperfections of daily life. A perfectionist might spend hours preparing for a presentation and then focus only on the one slide they stumbled over. They might ace an interview but lie awake, remembering the one question they could have answered better. Even success feels hollow because it never matches the perfect version they imagined. This feeling creates a cycle where achievements bring little joy, and the fear of imperfection grows stronger with each attempt to meet impossible standards.

Lack of Confidence

Lack of confidence often manifests as doubting one's abilities and self-worth, even when there's clear evidence one is capable. It might mean avoiding opportunities, second-guessing decisions, or assuming others have better judgment. You might find yourself apologizing before sharing your thoughts, using phrases like "this might sound silly, but..." or "I'm probably wrong, but..." to downplay your opinions.

These patterns worsen negative thinking because they create evidence that you do not belong and are not worthy, capable, or competent enough. When a colleague makes a casual comment, it automatically becomes proof of incompetence; you take simple mistakes and turn them into confirmation that you don't belong. Even success gets dismissed as luck or timing, creating a pattern where positive experiences slide away while negative ones stick. Your brain filters through reality and creates a sense of doubt, making it harder for you to recognize your strengths and capabilities.

Stress and Anxiety

An African proverb says that when the music changes, so dances. But in the grip of stress and anxiety, the music stays fixed on one harsh note. Our internal alarm blares constantly, unable to distinguish actual threats from imagined ones. Emails carry the weight of potential disasters. Deadlines loom like approaching storms. The brain rushes forward, spinning elaborate catastrophes from simple situations, believing that preparing for the worst will somehow prevent it.

Stress turns negative thinking into our default mode. A delayed message means we've offended someone. A quiet office signals impending layoffs. Even minor tasks tower over us like mountains. Our thoughts circle through worst-case scenarios, blocking out everything else. Each worry adds more stress, and each dose breeds more worries. Like water heating in a forgotten pot, the pressure rises until daily life boils over with imagined threats and constant fear.

Trauma

Trauma is a deep emotional wound that comes from experiencing or witnessing events that feel overwhelming or life-threatening. These can be significant events like accidents or abuse but also less apparent experiences like emotional neglect or constant criticism during childhood. When trauma occurs, it changes how the brain processes information and responds to the world around it. Think of it like a security system that gets permanently set to high alert—even when the danger is long past, the alarm keeps ringing.

Research suggests that repetitive negative thinking, including worry and rumination, is more common among adults who have experienced adverse childhood events, such as abuse or neglect. Repetitive negative thinking causes emotional disorders and worsens clinical outcomes, such as depression, suicidal ideation, PTSD symptoms, and cognitive difficulties.

This heightened state of alert leads directly to negative thinking. The brain stays prepared for the worst, scanning every situation for signs of danger. A person who experienced childhood bullying might interpret friendly teasing as an attack. Someone who lived through a natural disaster might feel intense anxiety every time dark clouds gather. The mind learns to jump to the worst possible conclusion because, at one point, that felt like the safest way to survive.

These thought patterns affect unrelated life areas. A harsh teacher's criticism can lead to avoiding any situation where evaluation might occur. A betrayal in a relationship can cause someone to see signs of abandonment in every interaction. The brain develops a quick-trigger response to anything that even remotely reminds it of past hurt, turning everyday moments into sources of anxiety and worry.

A stimulus acts as a trigger when it connects directly to the deeper patterns within us. Whether rooted in perfectionism, lack of confidence, stress, trauma, or experiences, our triggers light up these neural pathways like street lamps at dusk. They shed light on where our minds have learned to expect pain, disappointment, or failure. This connection between our triggers and their roots shows us the precise points where negative thinking has built its strongest defenses. The real work of change can begin at these points, where our triggers meet their source.

Environments and Emotional Experiences

Environments are peculiar because the same place that might've meant something a year ago could represent something entirely different. The office where you once felt trapped might now feel like a sanctuary from chaos at home. Your childhood bedroom that once symbolized safety might now stir up memories, you'd rather forget. A favorite coffee shop where you experienced heartbreak might transform into your favorite writing spot. Our surroundings shape our thoughts in ways we rarely notice, coloring our perceptions with layers of memory and meaning that shift like sand under our feet.

Our surroundings and emotions work together as architects of thought; they shape how we interpret and respond to every situation we encounter. The same environment can trigger entirely unique thought patterns depending on our emotional state, just as our emotions take on different colors depending on where we find ourselves. When confidence runs high, a networking event feels like a field of possibilities, but that same event, through the lens of anxiety, transforms into an emotional minefield.

The physical spaces we move through hold equal power over our thought patterns, often working silently to shape our mental state without our awareness. A cluttered desk amplifies scattered thinking while creating more mental noise, whereas an organized space helps create more apparent thought patterns and calmer responses to daily challenges. Lighting, sound, and social context affect our emotional responses and information processing. This constant interaction between our inner and outer worlds creates the foundation for thinking, reacting, and making sense of our daily experiences.

Breaking the Cycle of Negative Patterns

How do we move forward? It's easy—take a step, put one foot in front of the other, and will yourself to move. The path through negative thinking patterns works similarly—through small, deliberate steps that gradually create new ways of responding to our triggers. Like learning any new skill, changing our thought patterns requires patience, practice, and, most importantly, a clear understanding of where we want to go.

Four essential practices help us navigate this path:

- We name and refuse to shame our negative thoughts.

- We search for the source of our triggers with curiosity rather than judgment.

- We learn to work with our inner voice instead of fighting against it.

- We develop the ability to recognize and express our emotions openly.

These practices work together, each supporting and strengthening the others as we build new mental habits.

We design each practice for a specific purpose, but they are most effective together. Just as a carpenter knows when to use a hammer versus a screwdriver, we can learn which tool best fits each situation. Some days, we need to focus on naming our thoughts without judgment, while others, we need to dig deeper to understand their source. The key lies in developing all these skills gradually, knowing we can reach for the right tool when we need it most.

Name and Refuse to Shame

Learning to name our thoughts strips them of their hidden power. By stating, "I notice I'm having the thought that I'll fail," instead of just saying, "I'll fail," we create distance from the thought. This space allows us to see our negative thinking for what it truly is—a pattern, not a truth. Refusing to shame ourselves for these thoughts matters as much as naming them. Everyone has negative thoughts, showing where our mind needs more support and understanding.

Find the Source

Our triggers always point to something more profound. When a casual comment from a colleague sends us into a spiral of self-doubt, the actual issue rarely lies in the comment itself. By tracking our reactions back to their source, we often discover old wounds or unmet needs hiding beneath the surface. This exploration helps us understand why certain situations affect us so strongly, making our reactions more manageable and our responses more conscious.

Work With Your Inner Voice

Fighting against negative thoughts only makes them louder. Instead of trying to silence our inner critic, we can learn to engage with it differently. Acknowledging its presence without giving it the last word allows us to insert our conscious control. Our inner voice often tries to protect us, albeit in outdated ways. By understanding this, we can transform its role from harsh critic to helpful advisor.

Practice Knowing and Showing Emotions

Many of us learn early to hide or deny our challenging emotions. This creates a pressure cooker effect, where unexpressed feelings fuel negative thinking patterns. Learning to recognize and express our emotions helps us release this pressure. Simple practices like naming our feelings throughout the day or sharing them with trusted friends build our emotional vocabulary and confidence. As we become more comfortable with our emotional landscape, negative thoughts lose their grip on our minds.

Change happens in our small decisions in quiet moments when no one else is watching. It surfaces during mindful pauses or redirection of negative thoughts. These moments might seem insignificant, but they mark the beginning of a new relationship with our thoughts, one that is built on understanding rather than fear.

These patterns of negative thinking, once recognized and understood, become the raw materials for building mental resilience. We will continue to explore the practical tools and strategies that transform this understanding into unshakeable mental strength—the kind that helps you not just survive life's challenges, but thrive through them. Stay present, stay curious, and keep moving forward. Inner peace comes from accepting our thoughts, not fighting them.

Chapter Two

Cognitive Behavioral Strategies

Mental resilience isn't built through avoiding difficult thoughts—it's built by learning to work with them skillfully. The cognitive-behavioral strategies in this chapter are like mental training exercises that strengthen your ability to handle whatever thoughts and emotions arise. Each technique builds your mental resilience toolkit, giving you practical ways to bounce back stronger from setbacks and challenges.

At 3:47 A.M., Maria stares at her bedroom ceiling, her mind racing through tomorrow's presentation for the fourteenth time. She knows every slide by heart and has practiced her talking points until the words blur together, yet her thoughts keep circling back to everything that might go wrong. Down the hall, her teenage son Lucas lies awake, too, scrolling through social media and feeling the weight of every perfectly curated post from his classmates. Next door, Tom practices his "what ifs".

Three different people, three fresh worries, all caught in the same trap of thoughts spinning out of control. We often imagine our mental struggles as uniquely our own, carrying them like secret burdens.

Yet, it's important to remember that millions of people, just like you, wrestle with the same challenging patterns of thought in offices, homes, and coffee shops worldwide. Some count backward from one hundred to quiet their racing minds. Others make endless lists of pros and cons, hoping logic will silence their doubts. Many push through, believing this mental tug-of-war represents their natural state.

Most people never realize that these thought patterns follow predictable routes, like well-worn trails through a dense forest. While we might think of our thoughts as wild and uncontrollable, they actually respond to specific strategies—practical tools that can help us navigate even our most challenging mental terrain. These aren't quick fixes or empty positive thinking exercises, but tested approaches that help us understand and redirect our thoughts with purpose and precision. These are the fundamental building blocks of mental resilience—the ability to think clearly and respond wisely, even under pressure.

Cognitive Restructuring for Beginners

Mark sits in his office, staring at an email he must send to his team. He had received his promotion to project manager, a role he'd wanted for three years. Now, faced with his first team announcement, his mind fills with doubts. "They'll think I'm not qualified enough," he thinks. "I'll probably mess this up like that presentation last month." He's been sitting here for forty-five minutes, rewriting the same three sentences. Down the hall, his colleague Rachel faces her battle with a client proposal. "They'll see right through me," she tells herself. "Everyone else writes better proposals than I do."

These moments happen everywhere, all the time. In boardrooms and classrooms, at family dinners and job interviews, people get stuck in patterns of negative thinking that feel unbreakable. The thoughts come automatically: I'm not good enough, I'll fail, and everyone else is better at this. We accept these thoughts as truth because they feel authentic in the moment.

This is where cognitive restructuring makes a significant difference. At its core, it's a practical way to examine our thoughts and find better ways to respond to situations. It's not a complex or abstract concept, but a straightforward tool that helps us analyze our automatic negative thoughts and ask: Is this true? What evidence do I have? What advice would I give a friend?

Take Mark with his email; when he stops to examine his thoughts, he can see that his team has always responded well to his ideas. His promotion came after three years of solid performance. What about the presentation he thinks he messed up last month? His boss praised his recovery after the technical difficulties. He sees his situation more clearly when he looks at the complete picture, not just the negative parts.

The Process of Restructuring Thoughts

The process works in steps. First, we notice the negative thoughts when they show up. Then, we examine them, looking for the facts that either support or challenge these thoughts. Finally, we work on creating a more balanced view of the situation. This isn't about forcing positive thinking but finding a middle ground between harsh self-criticism and reality. It's about treating ourselves with the same kindness and understanding we would offer a friend in a similar situation.

Learning to restructure our thoughts means catching ourselves when we jump to conclusions, assume the worst, or turn one minor mistake into proof of complete failure. But with each practice session, with each thought we examine, we build a stronger foundation for handling life's challenges.

Step One: Catching the Thought

We start by simply noticing when negative thoughts appear. These thoughts often come with physical signals like a tightening in the chest, a racing heart, and shallow breathing. Failure thoughts might fill your mind while you prepare to give a presentation. Instead of getting caught up in the thought, you learn to pause and say, "I notice I'm having the thought that I'll fail." This slight shift creates space between you and the thought.

Step Two: Gathering Evidence

Once you've caught the thought, examine it like a detective. What facts support this thought? What facts challenge it? If you're thinking, "I always mess up presentations," ask yourself: Have you messed up every presentation? What about the times you did well? What about the positive feedback you've received? Write specific examples on both sides.

Step Three: Creating Balance

With the evidence in front of you, create a more realistic view. Instead of "I'll definitely fail this presentation," you might think, "I feel nervous, which is normal. I've prepared well and handled challenges before." This balanced thinking acknowledges both your concerns and your capabilities. It gives you a solid foundation for moving forward instead of staying stuck in fear.

Step Four: Taking Action

The final step moves you from thought to action. With a more balanced view, you can focus on practical steps. What would help you feel more prepared? It could practice with a friend, reviewing your notes more, or remembering past successes. These actions come from a place of self-support rather than self-criticism.

Through regular practice, this process becomes more natural. You learn to catch negative thoughts earlier, examine them more quickly, and find balanced perspectives more easily. The goal isn't to eliminate negative thoughts—they keep us alert and prepared. Instead, we learn to work with our thoughts in ways that help rather than hinder us. It's one of the most powerful tools for building cognitive resilience—the mental strength to question unhelpful thoughts rather than being controlled by them.

Challenging Automatic Negative Thoughts

Learning to challenge automatic negative thoughts is like building mental muscle—it strengthens your resilience and gives you more control over your emotional responses.

Alex stands in front of his bathroom mirror at 6:45 A.M., rehearsing his morning meeting presentation. He knows the material inside out and has prepared for weeks. The data supports every point he plans to make. Pre-event jitters hit: "They'll see through me," "I'll freeze," "I'll be stumped."

Our minds produce thousands of thoughts each day. Most float by like clouds, barely noticed. But some thoughts—the ones telling us we're not enough, we'll fail, we don't belong—these thoughts stick. They show up uninvited, plant themselves firmly in our minds, and start redecorating the place with worst-case scenarios. We call these

Automatic Negative Thoughts, and they affect everyone from seasoned executives to first-year students.

Understanding Automatic Thoughts

These thoughts appear without warning and often follow familiar patterns. The perfectionist hears, "This needs to be flawless, or it's worthless. People-pleasers often feel compelled to be nice. The overthinker gets caught in, "But what if everything goes wrong?" These patterns become so familiar that we stop questioning them. We accept them as reality rather than what they really are—habitual thought patterns we can learn to challenge.

The good news is that once we understand how these thoughts work, we can handle them differently. Think of automatic thoughts like pop-up ads in your mind. Just because they appear doesn't mean you have to click on them, and just because they sound convincing doesn't mean they're telling the truth.

Questioning What Feels True

Questioning these thoughts takes practice, but it starts with simple steps. When you catch an automatic thought, ask yourself:

- What actual evidence supports this thought?
- What evidence challenges it?
- How would I view this situation if it happened to someone else?
- How might a more neutral perspective help?

Take Alex and his presentation. When he stops to examine his thoughts, he remembers that his "freezing up last time" was just a five-second pause to pull up a specific data point. His fear of questions he can't answer overlooks his deep knowledge of the subject and his ability to say, "I'll find out and get back to you" when needed.

Building New Habits

The key to handling automatic thoughts lies in practice. Start small. Pick one common negative thought and track it for a week. Notice when it shows up, what triggers it, and how it affects your behavior. Please write the evidence for and against it. Look for patterns. Each time you question these thoughts, you build the mental equivalent of muscle memory.

Certain situations trigger these thoughts more often—high-stakes meetings, social gatherings, and performance reviews. This awareness itself becomes a tool. When you know your trigger points, you can prepare to handle automatic thoughts before they take over. You might create a list of your past successes to review before essential meetings or develop a quick routine for grounding yourself when social anxiety kicks in.

Reframing Your Inner Dialogue

Your inner dialogue shapes your mental resilience more than almost any other factor. When you learn to speak to yourself with strength and compassion, you build an unshakeable foundation for handling life's challenges.

Consider your intuition briefly. That constant commentator on your life might sound like a harsh critic, a worried parent, or an unsupportive friend. To Sarah, a graphic designer, it sounds like her old art teacher was always pointing out what could be better. Marcus, a new father, it echoes his own dad's critical tone. Elena starting her own business is a chorus of doubts that grow louder with each decision she faces.

This voice, our inner dialogue, is a powerful force that shapes how we navigate the world. It influences our responses to both minor daily hurdles and major life aspirations. The empowering truth? We have the ability to transform this voice, turning it into a supportive ally rather than a critical adversary. This process, known as reframing, begins with the realization that our thoughts are not immutable truths—they are malleable habits that we can reshape at will.

Changing the Conversation

Consider internal dialogue during setbacks. You may make a mistake during a presentation and immediately think, "I'm terrible at this. I should give up." This harsh self-talk feels natural because we've practiced it for years. Picture yourself advising a friend on a repeated mistake. You could say something like, "Hey, everyone stumbles sometimes. Remember how well you handled the questions afterward?"

This gap between how we treat others and ourselves shows us where to start. Reframing isn't about forcing positive thinking or pretending everything is fine. Instead, it's about finding a middle ground between harsh criticism and realistic encouragement. When you catch yourself saying, "I'm terrible at this," try, "I'm still learning. What can I do better next time?"

Building Self-Compassion

For most of us, it's easier to extend compassion to others than to ourselves. We can empathize with a friend's struggles, yet we demand perfection from ourselves. Breaking this cycle brings a sense of relief, as we learn to treat ourselves with the same understanding we offer others. This doesn't mean lowering our standards—it means acknowledging our shared humanity.

Some practical ways to build self-compassion:

- When facing a challenge, ask yourself: "How would I support a friend in this situation?"

- Replace "I should" statements with "I choose to" or "I'm working on."

- Acknowledge effort, not just results: "I tried something difficult today."

- Remember that struggling doesn't mean failing—it means you're growing.

Making the Change Stick

Changing your inner dialogue takes practice. Start by noticing when your inner critic shows up. What situations trigger it? What does it say? Write these moments down. This helps you spot patterns and prepare for them. Then, practice alternative responses. If your inner voice says, "You'll never figure this out," try. "This is challenging, but I can take it step by step."

Use specific situations as practice grounds for your inner dialogue. For example, when sending an important email, providing feedback to a team member, or trying something new, prepare some supportive phrases beforehand. Instead of thinking, "Don't mess this up," try telling yourself, "I've prepared well, and I can handle this."

These new thought patterns may feel awkward at first, much like writing with your non-dominant hand, but with practice, they will become more natural.

Your inner dialogue will evolve as you give it the space to change. The words you choose shape the actions you take. When you notice that critical voice starting up, pause, take a breath, and pick a different way to speak to yourself. The more you practice this pause, this choice, and this shift in language, the more automatic it will become. It is that simple.

Overcoming the Fear of Failure Through Self-Compassion

Self-compassion isn't just kind—it's one of the most resilience-building practices you can develop. It helps you bounce back faster from setbacks and face new challenges with greater confidence.

The email sits unopened in James's inbox. Subject line: "Feedback on Q4 Project." His heart races a little faster every time he sees it. Three hours have passed. Even so, he can't bring himself to click. Emma stares at a half-finished novel draft down the hall, cursor blinking on the empty page. The words used to flow easily, but since that harsh review of her first book, starting something new feels like walking through quicksand. Across town, David rehearses how he'll tell his family about his recent job loss, imagining disappointment on their faces before he's even spoken a word.

Fear of failure shows up in these quiet moments. It makes us avoid feedback that might help us grow, turns exciting opportunities into threats, and convinces us that every mistake carries permanent consequences. But here's what most people miss about failure: it hurts most when we face it alone, without compassion for ourselves.

The Power of Self-Compassion

We typically know how to console friends facing adversity. We remind them that setbacks are normal, help them see the bigger picture, and encourage them to try again. Yet, when we face our failures, this wisdom often vanishes. We become harsh critics, treating ourselves in ways we would never treat someone else.

Self-compassion means bringing that same friendly voice to our struggles. It means talking to ourselves like talking to someone we care about. This sounds simple, but it goes against years of believing that being hard on ourselves strengthens us or better.

Practical Ways to Build Self-Compassion

Start with small failures. When you make a minor mistake—emailing with a typo, forgetting someone's name, missing a turn while driving—notice your automatic response. Do you launch into self-criticism? Try catching yourself in these moments. Replace "I'm so stupid" with "Everyone makes mistakes sometimes." This practice, with minor setbacks, builds the foundation for handling more significant challenges.

Create a self-compassion routine for more significant setbacks:

- Acknowledge the pain. "This rejection letter really hurts."

- Connect with common humanity. "Many writers face rejection before success."

- Offer your support. "I'm proud of myself for trying."

The Results of Self-Compassionate Thinking

When you treat yourself with compassion after a setback, something remarkable happens. You bounce back quicker and glean more wisdom from the experience. You find yourself more willing to take calculated risks because you know that you'll support yourself even if things don't go as planned. This sense of growth and resilience is the fruit of self-compassionate thinking.

Think about a child learning to walk. They fall hundreds of times. But they never tell themselves they're bad at walking or that they should give up. They keep trying, supported by encouraging voices around them. We can learn to be that encouraging voice for ourselves.

Putting It To Practice

Start with situations that matter to you personally. Perhaps promotion application anxieties stem from a fear of rejection. You might have a business idea that stays locked in your notebook because "it's probably not good enough." Or you might dream of learning photography, but tell yourself you started too late.

Please take one of these situations and break it down into smaller pieces. Instead of "start a business," think "research five similar businesses this week." Rather than "become a photographer," focus on "learn three camera settings today." This makes both action and potential setbacks more manageable.

Now, create your self-compassion toolkit for these moments:

- **Morning Check-In:** Start your day by writing one thing you'll try, even if it feels uncomfortable. Add a note about how you'll support yourself if things don't go as planned.

- **Mid-Action Support:** When you feel yourself hesitating or pulling back, pause. Take three deep breaths. Remind yourself that discomfort means you're growing more assertive, just like muscles during exercise.

- **Evening Review:** Look at what you tried today. Write both the wins and the setbacks. For each setback, write what you learned and what you'll try differently tomorrow.

This practice gains strength through consistency. Keep a small notebook dedicated to tracking your experiences. Note the physical sensations that come with a fear of failure—the tight chest, the churning stomach, the racing thoughts. Familiarizing yourself with these signals helps you recognize when to activate your self-compassion responses.

When you stumble—and you will stumble—turn to this record. You'll see patterns emerge. You'll notice which self-compassionate responses work best for you. Most importantly, you'll build evidence to face challenges and continue, even when things don't go perfectly.

These cognitive-behavioral strategies form the backbone of mental resilience. By learning to work skillfully with your thoughts—examining them, reframing them, and treating yourself with compassion. You will develop the mental flexibility and strength that allows you to thrive through any challenge. In the next chapter, we'll explore how to build emotional resilience to complement these cognitive skills.

Chapter Three

Building Emotional Resilience

When you're five or six years old and learning to ride a bike, your entire world revolves around that moment. You remember your parents' comforting presence as you take those first wobbly rides. You trust them completely when they promise not to let go. Then suddenly, you move forward on your own. That supportive hand is no longer there, and for a split second, you feel like you're flying—until you're not. The concrete rushes up to meet you, and the sting of that first real fall burns through your palms, your knees, and your pride.

But then something remarkable happens. Through your tears, you see your parent's face, filled with a mix of concern and something else—faith in you. They don't rush to put the training wheels back on. They don't tell you that maybe bike riding isn't your thing. Instead, they comfort you, soothe your wounds, and ask, "Ready to try again?"

These early bike-riding lessons carry a truth that we often forget as adults: resilience isn't about never falling; it's about the people who help us stand back up, the voices that encourage us to try again, and, most importantly, the moment we choose to believe in ourselves. Over time, those supportive voices become our own. We learn to pick ourselves up and to trust that falling isn't the end of the story. However, somewhere along the way to adulthood, we expect perfection on the first try. Emotional wounds need care, like physical ones; life challenges require practice.

The Art of Emotional Resilience

The room falls silent when Maya walks in. Her team has just lost their biggest client, but her calm presence fills the space with steady energy. Later, someone will ask how she stays so composed under pressure. She'll smile and say, "I wasn't always like this." Ten years ago, the slightest setback would send her spiraling. Today, she navigates challenges with a grace that others notice. This isn't about natural talent or luck—it's about emotional resilience, a strength she built one difficult moment at a time.

Think of emotional resilience as your mind's shock absorber. When life throws you a curve ball—a rejected proposal, a relationship ending, a missed opportunity—this inner strength determines whether you stumble briefly or fall apart entirely. Some people seem to handle these moments effortlessly, but look closer. Their resilience comes from practice, facing more minor challenges and learning from each one.

Your Emotional Landscape

Your emotions tell stories about what matters to you. When criticism from your boss ruins your entire week, it might point to a more profound need for recognition. When a friend's success makes you feel hollow, it might reveal where you've put your dreams on hold.

Attention to these emotional signals helps you respond to life's challenges more effectively.

Start by getting curious about your reactions. Notice what situations make your chest tight, your shoulders tense, and your thoughts race. These physical clues often appear before you even realize you're stressed. Understanding these patterns gives you a head start on managing difficult moments.

Your Resilience Toolkit

Maya didn't develop her composure overnight. She started small—taking three deep breaths before responding to difficult emails, writing her thoughts when feeling overwhelmed, and talking to friends about her struggles instead of hiding them. Each practice added another tool to her emotional toolkit.

Try this: Next time you face a challenging situation, pause. Notice your immediate reaction. Ask yourself:

- What am I feeling in my body right now?
- What's my initial reaction to dealing with this?
- How can I feel more present?

The Power of Connection

Emotional resilience grows stronger through our connections with others. We often discover that others face similar challenges when we share our struggles. A colleague admits they also feel intimidated in big meetings. A friend confesses they too lie awake worrying about the future. These moments of honesty create bridges, turning personal battles into shared experiences.

Learning Through Stories

Every individual who effectively deals with setbacks has a tale of learning to overcome them. These stories remind us that resilience isn't about avoiding difficulty, but about growing through it.

Keeping Track of Growth

Start a simple practice: At the end of each day, write one challenge you faced and how you handled it. Some days, you'll write about significant victories. On other days, you'll note small moments of progress. Over time, these notes become a map of your growing strength, showing how far you've come and pointing toward where you want to go.

Remember Maya's team? They lost that client on a Tuesday. By Wednesday, they were already brainstorming fresh approaches, supported by her steady leadership. This wasn't just about bouncing back—it was about moving forward with purpose, using setbacks as stepping stones toward something better.

Tools for Emotional Regulation

There's an African tribe that believes emotions flow like rivers through the body. When a tribe member feels overwhelmed, the entire community gathers to sit with them to help their emotional waters flow freely again. They understand something many have forgotten—that our emotions need movement, space, and ways to flow naturally rather than building up like water behind a dam.

Movement: Your Body's Natural Reset Button

The young mother paces her living room at 3 a.m., gently bouncing her crying infant. Without realizing it, she's tapping into one of our most potent emotional regulation tools—movement. Her anxiety about the baby's distress eases as she walks. The simple act of moving helps mother and child find their way back to calm.

The movement works because it speaks the body's native language. When emotions flood our system—whether it's anxiety, anger, or deep sadness—they create physical tension like shallow breathing, tight muscles, or a racing heart. Trying to think your way out of these physical states rarely works. But movement? Movement creates change from the inside out.

Start with walking. Not the rushed walking you do between meetings, but intentional walking. Feel your feet meet the ground. Let your arms swing naturally. Notice how your breathing changes as you move. A ten-minute walk can shift your emotional state more effectively than an hour of worrying. Some people pace their living rooms during tough phone calls. Others walk around the block before making big decisions. The movement helps process the emotion, creating space for clearer thinking.

Stronger movement helps with stronger emotions. Put on music and dance in your kitchen. Do jumping jacks until your heart pounds. Run until your thoughts quiet down. These aren't just exercises—they're emotional release valves. Stress, disappointment, creative blocks—movement helps many process these emotions.

Even gentle movement carries power. Yoga, stretching, or simple shoulder rolls send signals through your nervous system that it's safe to relax. These movements work exceptionally well for emotions that make you want to curl inward and hide—sadness, shame, or feeling overwhelmed. The movement doesn't have to be perfect or follow any specific routine. It just needs to feel right in your body.

Create a movement menu for different emotional states:

- **Anxiety:** Rhythmic, repetitive movements, like walking or swimming.

- **Anger:** High-intensity movement like running or punching a pillow.

- **Sadness:** Gentle, flowing movements like stretching or swaying to music.

- **Feeling stuck:** Changing levels—lying, sitting, standing, jumping.

- **Overwhelm:** Simple, focused movements like arm circles or knee lifts.

Breath: Your Built-In Calming System

The presenter stands backstage, heart racing, palms sweaty. Five minutes until she faces an audience of three hundred. Her mentor taught her a simple trick years ago: breathe in for four counts, hold for four, and breathe out for four. As she follows this pattern, her racing thoughts slow. By the time they call her name, her hands have steadied. These tricks work because breath serves as a direct line to our nervous system—a line we can use anytime, anywhere.

Your breath changes with your emotions. Watch someone in anger—short, sharp breaths. In panic—quick, shallow breathing. In peace—long, slow breaths. But here's the fascinating part: just as emotions change your breathing, changing your breathing can shift your emotions. It works like a two-way street, giving you a tool that's always available, completely free, and surprisingly powerful.

Different breaths serve different purposes. When anxiety hits, lengthening your exhale sends safety signals to your brain. During moments of frustration, taking a deep belly breath creates space between the trigger and the response. For times when your focus is scattered, alternate nostril breathing helps you center your mind.

Some key patterns to practice:

- **Sleep:** The 4-7-8 breath (inhale for 4, hold for 7, exhale for 8).

- **Quick calm:** Box breathing (equal counts in, hold, out, hold).

- **Energy:** Sharp, quick inhales with long exhales.

- **Focus:** Alternate nostril breathing.

- **Overwhelm:** Simple belly breathing.

Mindful Presence: Becoming Your Observer

A father sits in a school meeting, hearing that his child struggles with reading. Old shame from his school days rises. But instead of getting defensive or shutting down, he notices tightness in his throat, heat in his face, and the urge to argue. Noticing these sensations—without trying to change them—helps him stay present enough to hear his child's needs.

Mindful presence means becoming curious about your experience instead of getting lost. It's the difference between being caught in a storm and watching the storm pass by. This doesn't mean detaching from your emotions. Instead, it means creating enough space to feel them without being overwhelmed.

Start with physical sensations:

- Notice where emotion lives in your body.
- Track how it moves or changes.
- Observe without trying to fix or change anything.
- Name what you notice: "There's a tension here," "Heat rising there."

Environmental Reset: Using Space to Shift State

Sometimes, changing your environment is the fastest way to shift your emotional state. The student who studies better at the library than in their messy room knows this instinctively. The employee taking tough calls in the stairwell rather than at their desk also understands it. Different spaces create different emotional possibilities.

Create designated spaces for different emotional needs:

- A calm corner for overwhelming moments.
- A movement space for processing potent emotions.
- A creative area for working through complex feelings.
- A comfort zone for self-soothing.

Small environmental shifts can make significant differences:

- Opening a window to let in fresh air.
- Changing the lighting.
- Playing specific music or creating silence.
- Adjusting temperature.
- Changing your body position.

Social Connection: The Power of Human Bonds

Late one evening, after a tough day at work, Samira calls her oldest friend. She doesn't need solutions or even advice—just someone to listen. As she shares her frustrations, her friend responds with small sounds of understanding. No fixing, no judging, just presence. By the end of the call, the day's weight feels lighter. This simple act of reaching out taps into one of our most potent emotional regulation tools—human connection.

We're wired for connection. Our nervous systems regulate better in the presence of someone we trust. Think about a child who falls and scrapes their knee. Their first instinct? Look for a parent. The sight of a caring face, the sound of a soothing voice, the feeling of being held—these experiences help their system return to calm. This need for co-regulation doesn't disappear as we grow up. It just takes different forms.

Building Your Support System

Think of your support system like different rooms in a house. Each serves a distinct purpose:

- The listeners who create space for you to process out loud.

- The humor-bringers who help shift your perspective.

- The truth-tellers who gently challenge your thinking.

- The comfort-givers who offer presence without pressure.

- The action partners who help you move forward when you're ready.

Not everyone needs to fill all roles. Some friends excel at listening, but struggle to challenge you. Others offer great practical support but aren't comfortable with deep emotional conversations. Knowing these distinctions improves timely communication.

Learning to Reach Out

It's common to hesitate when emotions are intense. We may worry about imposing on others or showing vulnerability, which can leave us feeling alone and without support. The inner voice repeats, "They have their own problems." "I should be tougher." "What if they see me as weak?" But remember, seeking support is not a sign of weakness; it's a display of strength.

But consider this: when a friend reaches out to you in difficulty, do you feel burdened? Or do you feel trusted, valued, and needed? Remember when someone confided in you? Remember how it deepened your connection and made you think, chosen, and trusted with something precious. Allowing others to support us strengthens relationships, creating deeper bonds through shared vulnerability.

Start small. You don't need to share your deepest struggles right away. Begin with everyday moments:

- Send a simple text: "Tough day. Could use a friendly voice."

- Share a small victory: "Finally finished that project, wanted to tell someone who'd get it."

- Ask for company: "Getting coffee later. Want to join? My treat."

- Express appreciation: "That conversation last week helped. Thank you."

Build regular connection points into your life. These routine check-ins create natural spaces for sharing:

- Monthly dinner dates with close friends.

- Weekly walks with a neighbor.

- Regular video calls with long-distance friends.

- Coffee meetings with a mentor or colleague.

- Group activities that foster natural conversation.

Find communities that embrace and celebrate vulnerability—where opening up is a strength. Sometimes, it's easier to open up in spaces specifically designed for sharing:

- Support groups focused on specific life challenges.

- Book clubs that discuss meaningful topics.

- Wellness or personal growth workshops.

- Online communities centered on shared experiences.

- Creative groups where people share their work.

Practice reciprocal support. When you show up for others, you create an environment where reaching out feels natural:

- Check-in with friends going through transitions.

- Remember and follow up on things they've shared.

- Offer specific help: "I'm going to the store—need anything?"

- Share your growth moments: "I learned something about myself today..."

- Celebrate their victories, no matter how small.

The more you practice reaching out, the more natural it becomes. Each act, no matter how big or small, of connection builds trust—both in others and in yourself. You learn that asking for support isn't weakness; it's wisdom. Sharing your struggles isn't burdening others; it's inviting them into a more authentic relationship. Being human together is, perhaps, the point of it all.

Learning the Language of Support

Different people need different kinds of support. Some need quiet presence, while others need active problem-solving with distraction and lightness. Pay attention to what helps you regulate. Can you put it into words? "When I'm anxious, it helps to have someone listen without trying to fix things." This emotional clarity makes it easier to ask for what you need.

Remember the African tribe we started with? They understood something essential—that emotions need witnesses, that healing happens in the community, that we're stronger together than alone. In our modern world, we might not have an entire village gathering when we're distressed, but we can create our circles of support, one connection at a time.

Building Your Resilience Journal

Words hold power. Writing "I feel overwhelmed" already creates a tiny space between you and that feeling. When you write, "This feels impossible right now, but..." you open the door to possibility. Each word you put on paper becomes a step back from the chaos of your thoughts, a way to see your emotional landscape differently.

Picture your mind like a city at night, glowing with many thoughts and emotions. From the street level, everything feels intense, immediate, and overwhelming. But write it down, and suddenly, you're looking at that same city from a hilltop—you can see patterns, connections, and quiet spaces you missed before. This is what a resilience journal offers: perspective.

Creating Varying Entries

Your journal can hold different forms of reflection:

Pattern Tracking: Notice and write:

- At what times of day do you experience peak and dip in energy levels?
- Which people lift you or drain you?
- How different environments affect your mood.
- What activities help you reset when stressed?

Celebration Pages: Record moments of resilience:

- Times you handled a situation better than expected.
- Small wins that show your progress.
- Difficult conversations you navigated well.
- Challenges you faced and overcame.

Growth Notes: Track your learning:

- What succeeded today that previously failed?
- Which old patterns are you outgrowing?
- What new strategies are you discovering?
- How are you different from six months ago?

Your Journal Is a Tool

The real power of journaling emerges in how you use it. During challenging moments, your past entries become a map showing paths you've already walked and challenges you've already faced. They remind you of the strength you sometimes forget you have. Your journal becomes evidence of your growth, proof that you can handle difficult things, and a record of how far you've come.

Let your entries be real. Some days might hold angry scribbles, other's peaceful reflections or hopeful plans. Write questions you can't answer yet. Note effective versus ineffective strategies. Note the moments when you surprise yourself with your resilience. Each entry adds another layer to your understanding of yourself; it builds a foundation for moving forward with greater awareness and strength.

It is far easier to believe that we will always feel this broken, this overwhelmed, this unable to cope. In our darkest moments, when emotions crash over us like waves, resilience can feel like a distant shore we'll never reach. We look at others who seem to navigate life's storms with grace and assume they were born with something we lack, gifted with an inner strength that passed us by.

Emotional resilience develops during quiet moments amid storms by taking deep breaths during anxiety, seeking support in darkness, and showing self-kindness in tough times. Each time we choose to move forward, breathe through the pain, write our fears, and share our struggles, we build something lasting within ourselves. Not an unbreakable wall, but a deeper understanding of our capacity to heal, grow, and rise again.

Chapter Four

Overcoming Self-Doubt and Inner Criticism

Self-doubt is one of the greatest enemies of mental resilience. It weakens our ability to bounce back from challenges and undermines our confidence in facing new situations. But here's the empowering truth: every time you learn to question your inner critic and speak to yourself with compassion, you're building confidence and resilience. The unshakeable self-trust that helps you thrive no matter what obstacles arise.

But I am not like her. I am not pretty enough or as sociable and as soft and tender-hearted as she is. Oh wow, he is so much smarter than me. The way he speaks in meetings, how he always knows exactly what to say. Observing them, one can sense their confidence and certainty about their role in the world. While here, I'm still questioning if I belong in this room.

These thoughts run through our minds like a familiar song played on repeat. They appear in job interviews, first dates, team meetings, and family gatherings. We hear them when we're about to try something new or when we catch our reflection in a store window. They keep us company late at night when we scroll through social media, comparing our behind-the-scenes footage to everyone else's highlight reel.

Self-doubt speaks in many voices. Sometimes, it sounds like our high school teacher who said we weren't college material. Other times, it mimics that parent who meant well but was always pushing for perfection. Most often, it sounds like our voice, but sharper, colder, and more confident of our flaws than our strengths. This inner critic sets up shop in our minds, appointing itself as the narrator of our story, pointing out every misstep, every awkward moment, every reason we might fail.

The problem isn't just that we have these thoughts—it's that we believe them. We accept their running commentary as truth rather than what it is: a collection of fears, old wounds, and protective instincts that no longer serve us. We rarely question the narratives defining our potential. But when we learn to see through these patterns and build stronger self-trust, we develop the confidence resilience that becomes unshakeable.

Identifying Your Inner Critic

Understanding your inner critic is the first step toward building genuine confidence resilience—the mental strength to trust yourself even when that critical voice tries to tear you down. That voice shows up right before your big presentation. You've prepared for weeks, and you know your material inside out, but there it is, whispering: "They're going to see right through you." It appears in the mirror when you're getting ready for a date: "You're not attractive enough." It rises during job interviews: "Everyone else is more qualified." This voice—your inner critic knows all your soft spots, old wounds, and places where doubt lives.

Think of your inner critic as a character in your story. Maybe it sounds like that teacher who said you'd never amount to much. Or that parent who pushed you to be perfect. Or that friend group that made you feel like you never entirely belonged. Over time, these external voices become internal, playing on repeat in your mind until they feel like your own thoughts.

Your critic shows up most often during moments of stretch and growth when you're about to try something new when you're putting yourself out there. When you're taking a risk, that matters to you. The voice gets louder when you're tired, when you're stressed, or when you're facing something that reminds you of past struggles. Pay attention to these patterns—they tell you something important about where your critic comes from and what it's trying to protect you from.

The hard truth? Your inner critic was probably helpful once. If you grew up in an environment where being perfect kept you safe, where making mistakes had real consequences, standing out meant standing alone—that critical voice helped you survive. It kept you alert, careful, and protected. Now, the voice adheres to outdated rules that are no longer relevant. It's like having an oversensitive smoke alarm that goes off at the slightest hint of steam—what once protected you now gets in your way.

Start noticing when your critic appears:

- Before important meetings or presentations.

- During social gatherings or networking events.

- When comparing yourself to others.

- While trying something new or challenging.

- In moments of visibility or recognition.

Notice also what makes it louder:

- Lack of sleep or self-care.
- High-stress periods at work.
- Conflict in relationships.
- Times of transition or change.
- Moments that remind you of past failures.

Your inner critic isn't the enemy, but more like an overprotective friend who never got the message that you've grown up. Understanding this helps you work with it rather than against it. When you hear that voice rise, you can acknowledge it: "I hear you trying to protect me, but I've got this." This simple recognition often takes some of its power away, letting you move forward despite its protests.

Tools for Quieting Self-Doubt

These tools don't just quiet self-doubt—they build lasting confidence resilience that grows stronger with each use. The meeting starts in twenty minutes. Your heart pounds as you review your presentation one last time. The familiar voice pipes up: "You're not ready. You'll mess this up." But this time, instead of letting these thoughts spiral, you pause. Take a breath. Notice these thoughts without getting tangled in them. This is mindfulness in action—not fighting with your doubts, but watching them move through your mind like weather patterns.

Training Your Mind to Work With You

Your mind can be your strongest ally or your most formidable opponent. Self-doubt often wins because we take its arguments at face value, accepting every criticism as fact. But what if you treated these thoughts like a scientist examining a hypothesis? When your mind says, "You can't excel at this," take a break. Get curious. Look for the gaps in this thinking.

Start by creating a distance between you and these thoughts. Instead of "I'm not qualified enough," try "My mind is thinking I'm not qualified." This slight shift changes everything—suddenly, you're observing the thought rather than being consumed by it. You become the researcher rather than the subject.

Then, dig deeper. Challenge each doubt with specific questions:

- "What evidence supports this thought?"

- "What experiences contradict it?"

- "If this happened to someone else, how would I interpret this situation?"

- "How would a supporter describe this situation?"

- "Is this thought helping me grow or holding me back?"

Keep a doubt diary for one week. Write every self-critical thought that appears. Next to each one, note what triggered it and what evidence exists for and against it. Patterns will emerge. You may notice self-doubt spikes after talking to certain people or during specific tasks. This knowledge gives you power—when you know what feeds your self-doubt, you can prepare for those situations with stronger mental tools.

Build a bank of counter-evidence. Each time you handle something well, write it down. When you receive positive feedback, save it. These become your weapons against future self-doubt. When your mind says, "You always mess up presentations," you can pull out concrete examples of times you have presented effectively. Your doubt loses power when faced with actual evidence of your capability.

Taking Smart Risks

Nothing silences self-doubt quite like proving it wrong. Start with small challenges that stretch you without breaking you. If speaking up in meetings terrifies you, begin by asking one question. If you dream of writing but fear judgment, share your work with a trusted friend. Each victory builds evidence against your self-doubt.

Please write these wins to keep track of them. When self-doubt whispers, "You can't handle this," you'll have concrete proof that you did hard things and survived. Your confidence grows not from empty positive thinking, but from the experience of your capability.

Being Your Own Ally

When you respond to a friend who is in the thick of disappointment, you listen. You remind them of their strengths. You help them see the bigger picture. However, when you are the one facing setbacks, this wisdom vanishes. Instead of offering understanding, you become your harshest judge. This pattern runs deep—we often save our sharpest criticism and coldest judgment for ourselves.

Breaking this pattern starts with recognition. Notice the difference between how you speak to others and how you speak to yourself. Would you ever call a friend stupid for making a mistake? You wouldn't remind someone every single time they've failed. Would you suggest they give up because they're "clearly not cut out for this"?

Creating a new inner voice takes practice. Start by catching the harsh words before they fully form. When you make a mistake, pause. Take a breath. Instead of launching into self-criticism, ask yourself:

- What would help me learn from this?

- How can I move forward constructively?

- What would I tell someone I respect if they were in this situation?

- What kind of strength did it require attempting this?

Build a personal support script for challenging moments like these:

"I faced something difficult today. Here's how I'm going to support myself through it..."

"This setback feels significant right now, but let me focus on what I can learn from it..."

"I choose to see this as information on what I can try differently next time..."

"My effort is more important than achieving perfect results..."

"I'm choosing to see this as information about what to try differently next time..."

"My effort matters more than perfect results..." Think of your inner ally as a mentor in training.

Like any new skill, supportive self-talk feels awkward at first. The critical voice might jump in, calling this approach soft or foolish. But remember—being your own ally isn't about avoiding reality or dodging responsibility. It's about creating an internal environment where growth feels possible, where mistakes become stepping stones rather than evidence of inadequacy.

Building New Patterns

Change happens in small moments, like when you question a self-critical thought rather than automatically believing it. In taking a risk instead of playing it safe. In offering yourself one moment of kindness instead of harsh judgment. Each time you make these choices, you create new neural pathways in your brain. The old patterns of self-doubt don't disappear overnight, but they gradually lose their power as you build stronger alternatives.

Constructing Positive Self-Talk

Positive self-talk is one of the most powerful tools for building confidence resilience. When you speak to yourself with strength and compassion, you create an inner foundation that can withstand any external criticism or setback. Audacity forms the basis of positive self-talk, believing in yourself despite doubt and being kind to yourself. It takes boldness to look in the mirror and choose words of encouragement over criticism, to face a challenge and say "I can handle this" instead of shrinking back.

This isn't about empty affirmations or pretending everything is fine. It's about building a new relationship with yourself, one honest conversation at a time. When you catch yourself thinking, "I'm not ready for this," pause. Consider what you'd tell your closest friend in the same situation. Would you list all the reasons they might fail? Or would you remind them of their strength, their preparation, their ability to learn and grow?

Start with small moments of truth. Before an important meeting, instead of rehearsing all the ways things could go wrong, try saying: "I bring value to this conversation." When facing a new challenge, replace "I'll probably mess this up" with "I can figure this out step by step." These aren't just word games - they're declarations of trust in yourself.

Build your positive self-talk muscle through practices like these:

- Keep a victory log of daily wins, no matter how small.

- Write compliments you receive, returning to them when doubt creeps in.

- Record moments when you surprised yourself with your own capability.

- Notice when negative self-talk shows up and consciously chooses a different narrative.

The power lies in specificity. Instead of generic phrases like "I am confident," try "I handled that difficult conversation well yesterday, and I can do it again today." Rather than "I am worthy," say "My ideas contributed value to our last project, and they will again." Ground your self-talk in authentic experiences, building a foundation of truth rather than dreaming.

Remember, positive self-talk isn't about ignoring reality or pretending challenges don't exist. It's about approaching these challenges with a mindset that serves you. When you face setbacks—and you will face them - positive self-talk helps you respond with resilience rather than resignation. Rather than attributing difficulty to lack of skill, the voice sees it as a chance to improve and grow.

Initially, speaking to yourself in this new manner may seem odd, possibly even unsettling. That's normal. Established routines, potentially longstanding, are being disrupted by you. But each time you choose encouraging words over harsh ones, you strengthen this fresh voice. Each time you speak to yourself with respect and possibility, you build evidence that you deserve your own kindness.

The Power of Seeing It First

Visualization builds confidence resilience by training your mind to expect success rather than failure. The more you practice seeing yourself succeed, the more natural confidence becomes in real situations. Athletes typically visualize their performance before every important competition. Before crucial surgeries, doctors mentally rehearse each step. Actors see themselves delivering their lines perfectly before stepping onto the state. This isn't wishful thinking—it's visualization, one of the most practical tools we have for building confidence and capability.

Think of visualization as creating a mental movie where you're the main character. Before that presentation you're worried about, take five minutes to see yourself walking into the room with purpose. Feel your feet on the ground. Notice your breathing. Is it calm? Picture yourself speaking clearly and handling questions with ease. This isn't about imagining a perfect performance—it's about familiarizing your brain with success, so it feels more natural when you're actually there.

Making Visualization Work for You

Close your eyes for a moment. Reflect on when fear hindered you from pursuing a desire. Hold that memory. Now imagine rewinding that scene and playing it again, but this time with a different ending—one where you move through the fear and take action. Feel the difference? This simple act of reimagining a moment is the essence of visualization. It's about expanding what you believe is possible by first seeing it in your mind.

Your brain is already running visualizations all day long. When fear or self-doubt takes over, it plays scenes of failure, embarrassment, and worst-case scenarios on repeat. Visualization practice is about taking control of this natural mental process and turning it from a source of anxiety into a tool for growth.

Choose your scene:

- That presentation you need to give next week.
- The job interview you've been preparing for.
- The difficult feedback you need to deliver to your team.
- The important conversation with your partner.
- The social event that usually makes you anxious.
- The creative project you've been hesitating to start.

Now build your visualization with precise detail. The more specific you make it, the more your brain treats it as actual practice.

Set the stage:

- Notice the room—its size, lighting, temperature.
- Who else is there? Where are they sitting or standing?
- What time of day is it? How does the light fall?
- What sounds are in the background?
- What tools and objects are necessary?

Place yourself in the moment

- Feel your feet planted firmly on the ground.
- Notice your posture—straight but relaxed.
- Feel your breathing—steady and calm.
- Sense the temperature of the air on your skin.
- Notice any tension in your body and let it soften.

Add the element of action:

- How do you enter the space?
- What are your first words?
- How does your voice sound—its tone, its pace?
- What gestures do you make?
- How do you move through the space?

Include interaction:

- How do others respond to your presence?
- What questions might arise?
- How do you handle unexpected moments?
- What support do you need, and how do you ask for it?
- How do you maintain your composure through challenges?

Define success in detail:

- What specific results show that this was a success?
- How do you feel afterward?
- What feedback do you receive?
- What did you learn from this experience?
- How does this success feel in your body?

Practice this when you're calm and focused. Begin with only three-minute intervals. As you get more comfortable, you can extend the practice, adding more detail and exploring different scenarios. The key isn't length—it's consistency and specificity. Each time you run through your visualization, you're creating neural pathways that make success feel more familiar and achievable.

The Power of Personal Truth Statements

Personal Truth Statements are the foundation of unshakeable confidence resilience—they ground you in your actual capabilities and achievements rather than fears and doubts. What is your truth? Not the harsh whispers of self-doubt, not the polite fictions we tell ourselves, but your real, lived truth. The truth of every challenge you've faced and overcome. Despite fear's attempts to halt you, you persevered through each moment. The truth of your resilience, your growth, your quiet victories that nobody else might see but that have shaped who you are.

This is where *Personal Truth Statements* begin—not with empty affirmations or idealistic notion, but with evidence from your own life. They're the stories you can point to and say, "This happened. I did this. This is who I am." While generic affirmations like "I am amazing" might feel hollow, statements grounded in your actual experiences carry the weight of truth.

Start by excavating your own history:

- What moments proved you were stronger than you thought?

- When did you surprise yourself with your own capability?

- What challenges have shaped you into who you are today?

- Which obstacles did you overcome that once seemed impossible?

- What qualities do those who know you best always recognize in you?

Now create statements that reflect these truths: Instead of: "I am powerful," Try: "Every time I've faced difficulty, I've found a way through."

Instead of: "Nothing can stop me," Try: "My track record shows I learn and grow from setbacks."

Instead of: "I deserve success," Try: "My efforts and persistence have created positive results before."

Your Personal Truth Statements should feel like putting on a well-worn jacket—comfortable, familiar, yours. They're not about pushing yourself to believe the impossible, but about reminding yourself of what you already know to be true about who you are and what you can do.

Making It Part of Your Day

Life moves fast. Juggling deadlines, responsibilities, and notifications can make self-care challenging, but the key is integrating these tools seamlessly into your daily routine.

What are the quiet moments already exist in your routine:

- Those first ten minutes after your alarm rings.
- The walk from your car to the office.
- The elevator ride to an important meeting.
- The pause before opening your laptop.
- The breath between receiving a challenge and responding to it.

These small spaces in your day are opportunities, so use that moment while waiting for your coffee to brew to see yourself handling an upcoming challenge. Let the time spent in traffic become a period to remind yourself of your capabilities. Turn your evening shower into a moment to acknowledge what you handled well today.

And look, sometimes you will forget; What matters is returning to these practices, letting them become as natural as checking your phone or taking a deep breath when stressed. Over time, you'll automatically reach and remember what you learned on your hard days. This is how genuine change happens: through small, consistent efforts of practice that are deliberately made a part of your day.

The aim is to live as your authentic self truly. Every moment you choose to question your inner critic, to imagine a new possibility, or to speak your truth, you're waking up to your power.

This journey through self-doubt isn't about becoming someone else; it's about remembering who you've been all along, beneath the layers of fear and hesitation that life painted over your confidence. These tools and practices can help unlock hidden potential within you.

The tools in this chapter aren't just about overcoming self-doubt—they're about building the kind of confidence resilience that becomes stronger with each challenge you face. Every time you question your inner critic, practice positive self-talk, or remind yourself of your personal truths, you're building mental resilience that will serve you for life. In the next chapter, we'll explore how understanding your anxiety triggers can further strengthen your emotional resilience.

Chapter Five

Understanding Anxiety Triggers

Anxiety triggers can feel overwhelming, but understanding them is one of the most powerful ways to build stress resilience. When you learn to identify what sets off your internal alarm system and develop skillful ways to respond, you transform anxiety from an enemy into valuable information. This chapter will teach you how to build the kind of stress resilience that helps you stay grounded and capable, even when life feels uncertain.

We've seen it in different forms, shapes, and intensities. Every morning, Michael checks his email seventeen times before opening any of them. Sarah rehearses conversations in her head for hours, mapping out how they might go wrong. David keeps three months' worth of savings just for "emergencies," then worries it's not enough and adds more. Anna says yes to everything, afraid that saying no might mean losing opportunities forever.

Seven-year-old Emma must check that her schoolbag contains everything thrice, even though she has taken nothing out. There's Dr. James, a surgeon with thirty years of experience, who still wakes up two hours before every procedure to go through his mental checklist.

There's Maya, the celebrated artist, who hasn't shown her latest work to anyone because "it's not ready yet"—for the past two years.

These aren't just habits or quirks. They're expressions of something more profound - responses to triggers that set off internal alarms. Each person's triggers are as unique as fingerprints, shaped by experiences, memories, and learned responses. Yet they all share a common thread: the desperate need to control what feels uncontrollable, to find certainty in an uncertain world.

Examine these patterns closely, and a map will emerge. Each trigger marks a spot where life once felt too overwhelming, where someone learned that staying on high alert felt safer than being surprised. These aren't character flaws or signs of weakness—their survival strategies that worked once but may not serve anymore. Understanding them involves more than just repairing faults. It's about building stress resilience—the ability to recognize triggers without being controlled by them, and to respond with wisdom rather than react with fear.

Identifying Personal Anxiety Triggers

Learning to identify your personal anxiety triggers is like creating a map of your stress responses. This awareness becomes the foundation for building lasting stress resilience—the ability to stay calm and capable even when triggers appear.

Jackson had recently broken up with his girlfriend of six years. He sat in the coffee shop, stirring his cold coffee, sharing his struggles with sleep and anxiety triggered by phone notifications and even simple tasks like ordering coffee. "Everything reminds me of her," he whispers. "The coffee shop we used to visit every Sunday. The shows we watched together. Even the way certain people laugh. It all brings her back. And it's not just missing her—every memory reminds me of what I lost and might lose again."

His experience opened up a much-needed conversation about triggers, moments, memories, or situations that set off our internal alarm systems. As he talked, his breakup had awakened older, deeper patterns of worry. His fear of abandonment stemmed from his parents' divorce—the pressure to always appear in control. To feel safe, he believes it is essential to plan for every outcome.

Where Our Triggers Come From

Every trigger tells a story. For some, like Jackson, it starts with a recent event that cracks open older wounds. Daily pressures can lead to its gradual development—seen in work perfectionism, parental anxiety, or test-related sickness.

These triggers often disguise themselves as rational concerns. Thoroughness is a way perfectionism disguises itself. "I need to be prepared" covers constant worry. "I'm being realistic" hides fear of failure. Identifying these patterns means looking beneath the surface and understanding what triggers us and why.

The Different Faces of Triggers

Our triggers fall into three major categories, each affecting us in distinct ways:

Internal triggers: These come from within—the thoughts and standards we set for ourselves. Familiar patterns include proving oneself at work, comparing oneself to others on social media, and aiming for perfection in decision-making. For the young manager who stays late every night, it might be the fear that leaving on time means she's not working hard enough. For the artist who never shares his work, it's the certainty that it needs "just one more revision."

External triggers: These are the situations and events we face daily. Some are obvious: job interviews, public speaking, meeting new people. Others are more subtle: the tension that creeps in during family gatherings, the dread of checking emails after a vacation, the stress of driving in heavy traffic. A teacher might feel it whenever she needs to meet with a challenging parent. A sales representative might experience it before every client calls, regardless of his years of experience.

Past experience triggers run deeper, shaped by memories and past events. Criticism of their ideas in school has made the person struggle to speak up in meetings. Someone who grew up with unpredictable parents might feel uneasy when plans change suddenly. The entrepreneur who lost money in their first business venture now hesitates to take even calculated risks. These triggers often feel more personal because they're connected to experiences that shape how we see ourselves and the world.

When We Track

When we track, we're teaching ourselves to recognize our struggles' true shape and size. Our minds often play tricks on us, making every trigger feel overwhelming and every reaction equally intense. But when we write things down, patterns emerge that challenge what we believe about our responses. We might discover that morning anxiety fades by lunch, certain people drain our energy more than others, or some fears appear right before important achievements. These realizations don't come from analyzing or judging—they come from simply paying attention and keeping records. Identifying our triggers helps us realize that "constant anxiety" has identifiable patterns we can learn to handle.

Start with a simple notebook. Each time you feel overwhelmed, take five minutes to write:

The situation:

- Time and place.

- What you were doing.

- Who was present?

- What happened right before?

Your response:

- First thoughts that came up.

- Physical reactions (racing heart, tight chest, sweating)

- What did you do next?

- How long did the feeling last?

Look for patterns:

- Does this occur during specific times of the day?

- Are particular people or places involved?

- What makes it better or worse?

- What helps you calm down?

Take Jackson's experience. Through tracking, he noticed his anxiety peaked not just when getting messages but any time his phone made a sound. Even work emails or texts from friends could trigger his anxiety - making him realize being triggered was not just related to his ex-girlfriend but also to unexpected communication.

Keep these notes for a few weeks. You'll see patterns—certain situations that regularly cause stress, specific interactions that make you uneasy, and times of day when you feel more vulnerable. This information becomes your guide for making changes, knowing when to prepare yourself, and understanding what kind of support you need in different situations.

Stress Reduction Through Mindful Living

Mindful living builds stress resilience by teaching you to work with difficult emotions rather than against them. When you learn to stay present during challenging moments, you develop the inner stability that makes you unshakeable.

We can learn from Buddhists that peace doesn't come from controlling our environment—it comes from learning to be present within it. While most of us rush through life trying to fix, change, or avoid what makes us uncomfortable, Buddhist practitioners spend years learning simply to sit with whatever arises. This ancient wisdom holds a powerful truth: our struggle with stress often comes not from our circumstances but from our constant effort to make things different from what they are.

You don't need to convert to Buddhism or spend years in meditation to take the valuable parts of the practice and integrate it into your life. It's about understanding a fundamental principle: that our minds create much of our suffering through resistance to what is. As humans, we may resist morning traffic by getting angry. Or resisting work pressure by worrying; we resist uncertainty through endless planning. Each resistance adds another layer of stress to our original situation.

The practice of mindful living offers a different approach. Instead of fighting against our experience, we learn to move through it with awareness. You don't have to accept everything passively or give up on change. Instead, it means learning to respond to life from a place of clarity instead of reaction.

Mindfulness is a lot like learning how to swim. Understanding water helps you float and move through it instead of sinking. Our stressful thoughts and feelings work the same way—fighting them may strengthen them while learning to move with them mindfully helps us find our way through.

Practical Ways to Live Mindfully

These mindful practices are like daily exercises for your stress resilience—small actions that build your capacity to stay centered no matter what's happening around you. Breath holds a sacred quality, as does your body's gentle reminder to remain present. Despite your mind drifting to future worries or past regrets, your breath is a reliable guide back to the present. It doesn't judge your wandering thoughts or try to fix your racing mind—it simply continues its rhythm, waiting for you to notice it again.

This same presence waits in ordinary moments throughout your day. It lives in the warmth of morning coffee against your palms, the sound of rain against windows, and the feeling of your feet meeting the ground with each step. These aren't just activities to get through—they're invitations to return to the present moment, to remember what it feels like to be fully alive in your own experience.

When you shower, let the water become your teacher. Feel its temperature on your skin, hear its sound, and notice how it travels down your body. When you walk, let each step bring you back to now. When you eat, taste your food, notice its texture, and experience each bite thoroughly. These aren't exercises for perfection—they're opportunities to practice returning to yourself repeatedly.

Moving With Mindful Awareness

The body loves it when you move and listen to the messages it sends. The body loves it when you take a moment to stretch, reach, and remember that you live inside this miraculous collection of muscles, bones, and breath. We spend so much time in our heads—planning, worrying, remembering—that we forget the wisdom that lives in our physical form.

Movement doesn't need to be complicated. Try lifting your arms or rolling your neck while sitting at your desk. It can be wiggling your toes inside your shoes during a stressful meeting, stretching your fingers wide, and making fists while waiting in traffic.

These movements act as entrances to the current moment. When thoughts tangle, and worries mount, your body offers a way back to now. Stand up. Stretch and feel the pull in your muscles, how your weight shifts as you move, and the subtle adjustments your body makes to keep you balanced. Mindfulness in motion requires no special equipment or perfect pose; you must acknowledge your existence beyond just a thinking mind.

Creating Mindful Moments

In the 2020s, there is an increasing fascination with romanticizing life moments. Users flood social media with posts about "main character energy" and finding beauty in morning coffee routines. It reflects the yearning to add meaning to mundane tasks.

But the actual presence goes beyond aesthetic photos of steaming coffee cups or perfectly arranged morning routines. It's about finding genuine moments of connection with your own experience. It's about transforming ordinary triggers into reminders to come back to yourself:

- Let red traffic lights become invitations to feel your breath moving in your body.

- When your phone rings, notice the weight of your feet on the ground.

- Before opening your laptop each morning, take three breaths to arrive fully.

- Choose one daily activity—making tea, washing dishes, walking to your car—to do with complete attention.

These bits and bobs of time are opportunities to remind yourself to step out of automatic pilot and into your life experience. Each reminder, pause, and moment of noticing is a small act of coming home to yourself.

The Practice of Coming Back

"Coming back" to yourself is perhaps the most important stress resilience skill you can develop. Each time you notice you've been swept away by anxiety and consciously return to the present moment, you strengthen your ability to stay grounded during future challenges.

Mallory sits across from her therapist, telling her she's returning to herself after what feels like eons. The therapist recognizes the significance of her reconnection to reality as a sign of closure and a new chapter.

The concept of "coming back" takes many forms. Sometimes, it's as simple as feeling your feet on the floor during a stressful meeting. Other times, it's catching yourself before the spiral of worry takes over:

- When overthinking keeps you up at night, focus on the feeling of your sheets against your skin.

- When anxiety builds before a presentation, count your steps as you walk to the podium.

- When family gatherings become overwhelming, excuse yourself for a two-minute bathroom break to feel your breath.

- When work pressure mounts, place your hand on your heart and feel its steady beat.

Like learning any new skill, coming back gets easier with practice. Start with one routine daily activity—brushing your teeth, waiting for coffee to brew, walking to your car. Make this your practice ground for presence. When your mind wanders to your to-do list or yesterday's argument, gently guide it back to the physical sensations of what you're doing right now.

Keep it simple:

- Set three specific times each day to check in with yourself.

- Use sticky notes with the word "breathe" as visual reminders.

- Create a gentle alarm on your phone labeled "Come back."

- Choose one daily task to do mindfully, even for just one minute.

The core purpose is to build a relationship with yourself based on patience rather than criticism. Each time you notice you've drifted away is a moment of awareness. Choosing to return is an act of self-care every time. We can build a sustainable practice—not through force or judgment, but through gentle persistence and understanding.

Understanding Your Mind Under Stress

Understanding how your mind works under stress is crucial for building lasting resilience. When you know what to expect from your anxious thoughts, you can respond to them skillfully rather than being overwhelmed by them.

The meeting hasn't started yet, but your hands shake as you arrange your notes. Next to you, your colleague appears perfectly calm while preparing for her presentation. Competing thoughts fill your mind: a missed typo on slide four, potential unanswered questions, nervous voice, upcoming deadline, and forgotten emails.

This is how the anxious mind works; it works in layers of thought piling up simultaneously. Each worry connects to another and creates a web of racing thoughts that can feel impossible to untangle. But, understanding this pattern is the first step toward working with it. For example, a tangled necklace needs patience and the correct technique to straighten out, so we can use specific approaches to sort out our thoughts.

The 5-4-3-2-1 Reset

This technique works because it engages all your senses systematically, pulling your attention away from anxious thoughts and into your immediate experience. It's powerful during moments when anxiety makes everything feel unreal or overwhelming. Here's how to use it:

- **Start with five things you see:** Take your time with this step. Don't just glance around—look. Notice the wall's texture, the way light falls across your desk, the colors in the room, the shapes of objects around you, and the patterns in your surroundings. Being specific helps: not just "I see a chair" but "I see a blue office chair with a small tear on the armrest."

- **Touch four things:** Feel different textures. Run your fingers across your clothing, touch the smooth surface of your phone, feel the roughness of a wooden table, and notice the temperature of a window pane. Pay attention to the specific sensations—is it smooth, rough, warm, cool, soft, hard? This step helps anchor you in your body.

- **Listen for three sounds:** Close your eyes if it helps. Listen for layers of sound—maybe the hum of an air conditioner, voices in the distance, or your breathing. Some sounds remain constant, while others fluctuate. Try to distinguish between nearby and far-away sounds.

- **Discover two scents:** The extra effort required is what makes it effective. Maybe it's the lingering scent of coffee, your hand lotion, or the surrounding air. If you can't immediately find a scent, try walking to another room or sniffing your sleeve. The act of searching for smells itself helps redirect your attention.

- **Focus on one taste:** Notice whatever taste is in your mouth. If you can't detect any taste, sip water or touch your tongue to your lips. Some people specifically keep a mint or piece of gum handy.

Progression is the essence of this exercise. When you move from five things to one, you're naturally narrowing your focus and creating a sense of order and control. It works best when practiced regularly, not just during intense anxiety. Try it during everyday moments—while waiting in line, riding the elevator, or sitting in traffic. This builds familiarity with the technique, making it easier to use.

Brain Dumping: Getting It All Out

Brain dumping builds stress resilience by clearing mental clutter and giving you perspective on your worries. When you get everything out of your head and onto paper, you often discover that many anxious thoughts lose their power. When your mind feels like a browser with fifty tabs open, this technique offers relief because everything comes out precisely as it exists in your mind.

How to Brain Dump Effectively:

Find Your Space

- Select a quiet moment when no one will interrupt you.

- Grab paper and pen (typing works too, but handwriting often helps access thoughts).

- Set a timer for 10-15 minutes.
- Put your phone on silent.

Write Without Rules

Start writing whatever comes to mind:

- The project deadline that keeps you up at night.
- The friend you need to call back.
- The weird pain in your knee you're worried about.
- The grocery items you're running low on.
- The argument you had last week.
- The email you forgot to send.
- The troubling dream you had last night.
- The random song lyric stuck in your head.

Don't:

- Organize your thoughts.
- Make it look pretty.
- Worry about spelling.
- Judge what comes up.
- Try to solve anything yet.

- Stop until your timer rings.

After the Dump:

Let it sit for at least an hour. When you return, you might notice:

- Patterns in your worries.
- Tasks that genuinely need your attention.
- Thoughts that seemed huge but looked smaller on paper.
- Things you can do something about versus stuff you can't control.

Now you can:

- Circle workable items.
- Cross out what's not essential.
- Group similar thoughts together.
- Choose what needs attention first.

Make it a regular practice:

- Start each morning with this quick process; clear your head.
- Use it before bed to help your mind let go.
- Try it when feeling overwhelmed at work.
- Use it before meaningful conversations or decisions.

Healing can be deeply uncomfortable, but would you rather spend your life avoiding the potential of who you could become? Every step toward understanding your mind and working with it instead of against it unlocks new opportunities. It's not about achieving perfect calm—it's about turning discomfort into a path for growth. The tools are available. The decision to use them is yours.

Understanding your anxiety triggers isn't about eliminating them completely—it's about building the stress resilience to handle them skillfully. Every time you practice identifying triggers mindfully, coming back to the present moment, or clearing your mind through brain dumping, you're strengthening your capacity to stay grounded and capable no matter what challenges arise. In the next chapter, we'll explore how positive psychology can further enhance your mental resilience by helping you build on your strengths.

Chapter Six

The Power of Positive Psychology

This question gave birth to positive psychology—the science of understanding what makes life worth living. It explores how to build something beautiful, how people find meaning in their circumstances, what allows communities to thrive, and what creates genuine happiness and deep satisfaction.

This is the stuff that joy is made of: Slow mornings when you wake up and realize that you don't have to rush anywhere. The sun is filtering through your curtains, and the quiet hum of the world is not yet fully awake. The luxury of stretching, letting your mind wander, feeling the warmth of your bed, and knowing you can stay there a little longer.

Everyday moments, like the steam from coffee and a favorite song playing at the right time, bring joy. Each day offers these glimpses of sweetness, these chances to pause and savor what makes us feel most human, most alive. By understanding these moments, we grasp what truly nourishes our well-being and helps us thrive rather than survive.

The practice of positive psychology opens up a different way of living. It teaches us to cultivate moments of joy deliberately, building them into the fabric of our days rather than waiting for them to appear by chance.

Understanding What Makes Life Good

For decades, psychology has focused on healing what hurts in our minds—depression, anxiety, trauma, and stress. It was like studying health by examining illness alone or trying to understand love by looking only at heartbreak. Then, in the late 1990s, a psychologist named Martin Seligman asked a simple but revolutionary question: What if we studied what goes right?

This question gave birth to positive psychology—the science of understanding what builds unshakeable inner strength. It explores how to cultivate lasting resilience, how people find meaning in their circumstances, what allows communities to thrive, and what creates deep resilience and lasting satisfaction.

Think of it like tending a garden. Traditional psychology worked on removing weeds—addressing problems as they appeared. Positive psychology looks at how to make things grow—what conditions create the best soil, what nutrients help plants flourish, and how to cultivate environments where good things naturally take root and grow.

This science draws wisdom from many sources. Brain researchers show us how practices like gratitude reshape our neural pathways. Sociologists reveal how solid communities build resilient individuals. Anthropologists help us understand how different cultures find and create meaning. Together, these perspectives paint a richer picture of human flourishing.

This approach offers practical tools for building mental resilience: ways to strengthen relationships, methods for finding more engagement in work, and practices for experiencing more joy in everyday moments. These strategies create lives rich in meaning, purpose, and genuine satisfaction. I found a transformative online course on Seligman's concepts, which I took years ago. I thought it was life-changing and sparked my interest in the subject.

The course's teachings suggest we can examine and change negative thinking patterns, which are not fixed traits, but learned responses. Several key insights emerge:

- Negative thinking often serves a protective function but can become maladaptive when overused.

- Positive psychology techniques can work alongside rather than replace realistic assessment of challenges.

- We can balance the brain's negativity bias by intentionally focusing on positive experiences.

- Personal growth often requires integrating both positive and negative aspects of experience.

Harvard's Positive Psychology course didn't suggest eliminating negative thinking entirely, but advocated for a more balanced psychological approach. The course's enduring popularity suggests that many people recognize the limitations of purely negative thinking patterns and seek evidence-based alternatives for achieving psychological well-being.

Growth resilience transforms how you approach difficulties—instead of viewing challenges as threats to avoid, you begin to see them as opportunities to strengthen your mental and emotional capacity.

Growing Through Life's Challenges

Think of your mind like a garden again, but focus on the gardener this time. To some gardeners, a dry patch of earth represents what will never flourish. Others look at the same patch and imagine possibilities—what could thrive with the proper care, patience, and understanding? This is the essence of a growth mindset: seeing potential where others might see limitations.

Maria used to believe she was "just bad at public speaking." Every presentation felt like evidence of this unchangeable fact. Then, something shifted. She started viewing each speaking opportunity as a chance to learn something new—about her voice, presence, and ability to connect with others. She began recording herself, noting what worked and what she could improve. Each presentation became an experiment rather than a test of her worth. Two years later, she leads workshops teaching others how to find their voice.

This shift in perspective changes everything. A colleague who gives constructive feedback becomes a valuable teacher rather than seen as a critic. The project that falls short becomes a masterclass in what to try differently next time. The new skill that feels impossible becomes an invitation to discover what persistence can accomplish.

The Power of Yet

There's magic in this tiny word "yet." It sits at the edge of possibility, transforming full stops into commas, endings into beginnings, and limitations into doorways. When we say, "I can't do this yet," we acknowledge our current reality and the potential for change. The struggle remains real, but it becomes temporary rather than permanent.

Think about how this shift in language reflects a shift in thinking:

- "I'm not good at relationships" becomes "I'm not good at relationships yet"—recognizing that emotional intelligence grows with experience.

- Changing "I always freeze during interviews" to "I always freeze during interviews yet" subtly suggests gradual confidence building.

- "I never stick to my goals" becomes "I never stick to my goals yet"—opening up the possibility of developing new habits.

- "Public speaking terrifies me" becomes "Public speaking terrifies me yet"—hinting at courage waiting to be discovered.

This simple word does something profound: it keeps our story unfinished. It suggests that where we are now is simply a chapter, not the entire book. When we add "yet" to our limitations, we allow ourselves to be honest about our struggles and hopeful about our capacity to grow through them.

Yet reminds us that discomfort in learning is normal, that confusion often precedes understanding, and that awkwardness usually comes before mastery. It stands as a bridge between who we are and who we might become, between what feels impossible today and what might feel natural tomorrow.

Learning to Learn

Growing through challenges requires us to become students of our own experience. Each difficulty, each moment of struggle, each setback carries a lesson within it—if we learn to look for it. This means developing new habits of mind and new ways of approaching challenges:

Start with questions when facing difficulties, pause and ask:

- "What assumptions am I making about my abilities?"
- "Where exactly am I getting stuck?"
- "What small step could I try next?"
- "Who might help me see this differently?"

Create Learning Rituals:

- Keep a growth journal where you track what you learn and how you learn.
- Write one thing you discovered about yourself each day.
- Review your progress weekly, noting patterns in what helps you grow.
- Document strategies that work for you, building your toolkit.

Build Your Learning Community; Surround yourself with people who:

- Share their learning journeys openly.
- Offer specific, constructive feedback.
- Celebrate your efforts, not just your outcomes.
- Remind you of your progress when you forget.

Break Down Barriers When Something Feels Overwhelming:

- Divide it into smaller, manageable pieces.

- Focus on one aspect at a time.

- Create milestones you can celebrate along the way.

- Track your progress in visible ways.

Remember Lisa, who started learning piano at forty-five? She put sticky notes around her house: "Your fingers feel clumsy because they're learning something new," and "Mistakes mean you're trying something challenging. It wasn't just the notes that mattered, but her approach that made the real impact. She broke down complex pieces into manageable sections. Then she recorded herself playing and listened with curiosity instead of criticism. She found encouragement and camaraderie in their shared journey by sharing her progress with a community of adult learners online. Six months later, she sang beautifully at her daughter's wedding, valuing growth over perfection.

Positive emotions are builders in your life. Each genuine smile, each moment of delight, each burst of curiosity, lays down another brick in the foundation of your well-being. When you feel good, you're more likely to start a conversation with someone new, try something challenging, and see possibilities where you once saw obstacles. These small actions, driven by positive feelings, create ripples. Conversations that lead to a friendship. The challenge teaches you something new about yourself. Possibilities that become reality.

Your body knows this wisdom, too. In moments of genuine happiness, your nervous system relaxes, your muscles ease, and your breathing deepens. While stress tightens and constrains, positive emotions create space—space to breathe, to think, and to heal. This explains why people who regularly experience positive emotions often sleep better, get sick less frequently, and even live longer.

But here's the beautiful part: you can cultivate these good feelings deliberately. It starts with paying attention to what already brings you joy. Maybe it's the first sip of morning coffee, how your dog greets you at the door, or the satisfaction of completing even a small task. When you notice these moments, pause. Let them fill you up. Let them last a few seconds longer than they usually would.

Savoring pleasant moments is like building compound interest. Each time you take a moment to fully enjoy a positive feeling, you make it easier to notice the next one. Over time, you train your mind to see the good around you, embrace it, and let it truly uplift you.

Start small. Notice one good thing each morning before you get out of bed. Take three deep breaths when something makes you smile. Share your moments of joy with others, letting the telling of it double your pleasure. These aren't just nice things to do—they're investments in your emotional well-being, creating resources you can draw on during more challenging times.

Building a Life of Meaning and Purpose

Meaning emerges from our daily choices, not from empty platitudes like "stay positive." True growth comes from allowing ourselves to fully experience our emotions, then consciously deciding how to channel them. We find purpose not through following prescribed formulas, but by connecting our actions to something greater than ourselves.

Finding Your North Star

The most fulfilling lives have direction. Think of sailors who used to navigate by the stars—they might take different routes and face different weather, but they always knew which light to follow. Your values work the same way. Decisions become clearer when you see what matters most—creativity, connection, learning, or service. Every choice either moves you toward or away from your personal North Star.

Some people find their direction early, like the child who always knew she wanted to heal others and grew up to become a doctor. Others discover it through experience, such as the corporate lawyer, who realizes his most profound satisfaction comes from mentoring younger colleagues, not winning cases. Some find it through loss, like the woman who transforms her grief into a foundation helping others. When you find what truly matters to you, you'll know it. It hits you with a sense of clarity - this is where your energy belongs. The specific way you get there isn't as important as recognizing it when you see it.

What drives you might seem simple to others. It could be making people feel at home when they walk into a room, sharing experiences that help others feel understood, or fixing problems that most people walk right past. What matters isn't how big or impressive your purpose looks to others - it's how deeply it matters to you.

When you're doing what you're meant to do, even the hard days feel worthwhile. Problems become puzzles to solve instead of roadblocks. And when you fail, you get back up because you know exactly why this work matters to you.

Finding this direction requires attention to what lights you up, what activities make time disappear, and what topics make you lean forward in conversation. It means noticing what you're good at and what feels meaningful, even when it's hard. Your North Star combines your natural gifts with the impact you want to have on the world around you.

The Power of Small Actions

Big dreams are important, but true meaning is found in small moments. It's the teacher who stays after class to support a struggling student. The artist who returns to their canvas each morning, regardless of inspiration. The friend who reaches out during difficult times. These small, intentional acts weave together a life filled with purpose.

Beyond Yourself

Something magical happens when we connect to more significant causes than our concerns. An environmental activist feels part of Earth's healing. The mentor watching their guidance shapes a younger person's path. A volunteer at a local shelter sees how their presence makes a difference. This connection to something bigger turns ordinary actions into meaningful contributions.

The shift happens gradually. A woman picks up trash during her morning walks and soon notices other neighbors joining her. Students who used to struggle end up helping younger kids years later. A man plants a community garden, creating food and a gathering place where strangers become friends. These actions ripple outward in ways we could never predict.

Some people find their larger purpose in obvious places—charitable organizations, community leadership, and social movements. Others discover it in quieter ways—the grocery store clerk who makes older customers feel less lonely, the bus driver who learns every child's name, the neighbor who checks on shut-ins during storms. The size of the action matters less than the intention behind it: the choice to see your role in the broader web of human connection.

Reaching beyond ourselves teaches us to see daily life in a new light. Mundane tasks take on new significance when connected to larger purposes. Filing paperwork becomes supporting families in crisis. Answering emails helps students find their path. Attending meetings becomes building a more sustainable future. When we understand how our small actions contribute to changes, even ordinary days feel extraordinary.

Using Your Unique Gifts

- What are you good at?
- What makes you want to jump out of bed in the morning?
- What problems do you solve so naturally that others come to you first?

These questions point toward your unique gifts—the talents that flow through you as naturally as breathing. Some effortlessly calm tense situations. Others can take complex ideas and make them simple enough for anyone to understand. Some have the patience to sit with an older adult and truly listen to stories they've told a hundred times before.

Notice the moments when time seems to shift. When are you so immersed in what you're doing that you forget to check your phone? When do you feel most alive, most like yourself? These moments often hold the key to your gifts, like the writer who loses hours in the flow of crafting stories. You might be the gardener whose hands instinctively know what each plant needs. We have all known those teachers who can sense the exact moment a student is about to understand a tough concept.

Finding Your People

There's so much to explore about community—the way we lean on each other, grow through each other, and discover ourselves in the moments that unfold between hello and goodbye. Meaning doesn't thrive in isolation. Shared spaces foster connections: book clubs, community gardens, volunteer groups.

The magic of finding your people lies in the recognition—the moment you realize you're not alone in how you think, dream, or see the world. These connections ground us, reminding us that our personal journeys are part of a larger human experience. Our lives gain richness and purpose when they intertwine with others.

It's easy to get stuck thinking that a meaningful life is for other people - the ones who seem to have everything figured out. You might tell yourself you're just someone who will always struggle with worry and self-doubt. Perfect people don't have a monopoly on meaning, and you don't need to solve all your problems before finding it.

You deserve to find purpose and joy simply because you're here, not because you've reached some imaginary standard of worthiness.

And by reading these words, you've already taken the first step toward embracing them. The practices in this chapter aren't just about feeling good—they're about building the deep resilience that carries you through life's inevitable storms. When you cultivate positive emotions deliberately and create meaning from your experiences, you're essentially building an inner fortress of strength that no external circumstance can shake.

Chapter Seven

Mindfulness and Meditation Techniques

Oh, how lovely it is to be a taker of space, a noticer of things, a feeler of emotions. How often do you allow yourself to be any of those things? How frequently do you permit yourself to exist in a moment without trying to fix it, change it, or rush through it? We live in a world that values doing over being, measures worth in productivity, and sees stillness as wasted time. We carry endless to-do lists in our pockets, wear devices that count our steps and measure our sleep, and fill every quiet moment with noise from our screens.

Our bodies know it when we pause to watch the snowfall, lose track of time listening to the rain, or find ourselves breathing in rhythm with ocean waves. These moments of natural mindfulness remind us we are more than our schedules and obligations. They whisper to us about a way of experiencing life, where we don't just pass through our days but truly inhabit them.

There lies a space between stimulus and response, thought and action, inhale and exhale. Mindfulness invites us to explore this space, to make our home there. It asks us to become intimate with our own experience, to cultivate curiosity about what it means to be fully alive at this moment, precisely as it is.

Understanding Mindfulness

Mindfulness started as a practice over 2,500 years ago, but its relevance to modern life has caught the attention of scientists, doctors, and mental health professionals worldwide. Dr. Jon Kabat-Zinn, who introduced mindfulness to Western medicine in the 1970s, defines it simply as "paying attention in a particular way: on purpose, in the present moment, and non-judgementally."

This practice shows up differently for different people. For some, it means sitting quietly and following their breath. For others, it means fully engaging in daily activities—feeling the warmth of water while washing dishes or noticing the taste and texture of each bite during meals. They pay attention to how their feet meet the ground while walking. The form matters less than the intention: to be present with whatever is happening without trying to change it.

Research from Harvard Medical School suggests that people spend nearly 47% of their waking hours thinking about something other than what they're doing Bradt (2010). This constant mind-wandering leads to stress, anxiety, and decreased satisfaction with life. Mindfulness offers an alternative—a way to fully take part in our own experience instead of always being somewhere else in our minds.

The practice requires no special equipment, particular beliefs, or specific location. It simply asks us to show up for our own lives, moment by moment. This might sound simple, but in a world designed to capture and scatter our attention, choosing to be present becomes a radical act of self-care.

Daily Mindfulness Practices

The best part about a new day is that it offers you a chance to start again. The past day's events may not completely fade away, but a new day presents a chance for a different approach. Here's how:

Start With a Morning Surrender

How you start your morning ultimately determines how the rest of your day will go. When you open your eyes in the first few minutes, set the tone for everything that follows. Claim these moments for yourself before reaching for your phone, checking emails, and letting the world rush in with its demands.

Start by connecting to your breath, allow yourself to defrost, and feel your body waking up. Notice the weight of the blanket, the texture of the sheets, and the quality of light in your room. Let this be your first act of consciousness—simply noticing you are alive for another day. Then, as you move through your morning routine, choose one activity to do with complete attention. Perhaps it's standing in the shower, feeling the water on your skin, letting it wash away yesterday's worries.

Make this practice concrete:

- Set your alarm 10 minutes earlier than usual.

- Keep your phone on airplane mode for the first hour.

- Choose to do one of your morning rituals (coffee, shower, breakfast) mindfully.

- Notice three specific things about this chosen activity.

- Let yourself fully experience these moments before the day begins.

These aren't empty rituals or forced meditation. They're acts of claiming space for yourself, of remembering what it feels like to move through life aware before the world's momentum carries you away.

Walk With Awareness

Walking is such an underrated form of connection, connection to the self, something greater than us, and something fundamental to being human. Every journey is a chance to move mindfully at your own pace.

Transform ordinary walks into moments of presence. Feel your body as you move through your day, whether you're walking to your car, catching the train, or stepping out for lunch. Pay attention to simple sensations - your feet touching the ground, the air on your skin, the way your body carries you through space.

These aren't special walks you need to add to your schedule; they're the ones you're already taking, just experienced more fully.

- Walking to your car after work.

- Moving between meetings.

- Taking out the trash.

- Getting the mail.

- Walking down the hall to the bathroom.

During these walks, choose this moment to notice:

- The rhythm of your steps.

- How your weight shifts from one foot to the other.

- The temperature of the surrounding air.

- The sounds are near and far.

- The way your body naturally knows how to move.

This practice doesn't ask you to walk differently or add anything to your schedule. It simply invites you to be present in the walking you already do, to remember that even the most mundane journey can become a moment of returning to yourself.

Eating as Practice

Food, there's so much to say about it; something that makes it more than mere sustenance. It carries the memories of childhood kitchens, celebrations shared with loved ones, and quiet moments alone with a warm cup of tea. Every meal offers an invitation to presence, a chance to notice not just flavors and textures but the simple miracle of nourishment.

Choose one meal a day to eat without distractions. No phone, no TV, no reading. Just you and your food. Notice the colors on your plate, the textures in your mouth, and the journey of each bite. This isn't about eating perfectly—it's about being perfectly present with whatever you eat.

Make this practice simple:

- Start with just the first three bites of a meal.

- Notice the temperature of your food.

- Feel the weight of your utensils.

- Listen to the sounds of eating.

- Observe how flavors change as you chew.

- Notice when you feel satisfied.

Even a simple sandwich eaten mindfully can become a moment of meditation. Even a quick breakfast can offer a pause in your day. The food itself matters less than your willingness to be present with it, to notice what's already there waiting to be experienced fully.

Evening Reflection

Just as we start the day ahead with intention, we have to choose how we end it deliberately. These final moments before sleep shape not only how we rest but also how we carry today's experiences into tomorrow. This isn't about forcing positivity or pretending the day was perfect—it's about pausing long enough to notice what happened, to acknowledge the life you're living.

End your day by noticing three things: something you saw, heard, and felt. Write them down or hold them in your mind. Notice simple things: a friend laughing, rain, your child's hand.

Create a simple evening ritual:

- Find a quiet moment before bed.

- Take three deep breaths.

- Notice where your body holds tension.

- Recall one moment of connection from your day.

- Remember one small joy.

- Acknowledge one challenge you faced.

This practice takes just a few minutes, but changes how you close each chapter of your life. It reminds you that every day, no matter how ordinary or challenging, holds moments worth noticing, worth honoring, worth carrying forward into tomorrow.

Finding Stillness Through Meditation

Your mind works like a snow globe—constantly swirling thoughts, worries, and plans. Meditation creates conditions where everything can naturally settle into place. Here are three approaches that have helped countless people find their way to inner quiet:

Guided Meditations:

Sometimes, we don't know where to start; we think about the whole concept of meditation and work ourselves into a state of overthinking what should be natural—the simple act of being present.

Let's start with a simple guided practice that you can return to at any time:

A Five-Minute Meditation to Ground Yourself

Find a comfortable position. You might sit in a chair with your feet flat on the floor or on the edge of your bed. Let your hands rest naturally in your lap or on your knees. Take a moment to adjust until you feel stable and at ease.

Now, take a deep breath in through your nose. Feel your belly expand like a balloon. Hold it for a moment. Then release slowly through your mouth, feeling your shoulders drop as you exhale. Do this two more times at your own pace.

Let your breathing return to its natural rhythm. Notice the air moving in and out of your body. Feel the weight of your body supported by whatever you're sitting on. Notice the points of contact—your feet on the floor, your legs against the chair, your hands where they rest.

As thoughts arise, and they will—imagine them as clouds passing across a vast sky. You are the sky; thoughts are just weather moving through. There is no need to push them away. Notice them passing.

For the next few minutes, rest your attention gently on your breath. When you notice your mind has wandered, bring it back to the sensation of breathing. Notice the rise and fall of your chest, the air moving past your nostrils, and the subtle movement of your belly.

Before opening your eyes, take one more deep breath. Feel the alertness in your body, the clarity in your mind. Carry this feeling of groundedness with you as you return to your day.

Remember, every time you practice this meditation, it might feel different. Some days, your mind will feel busy, and others will be quieter. All of these experiences are valid parts of the practice.

Progressive Relaxation: The Body's Way to Peace

Our bodies hold stories in every muscle. That knot in your shoulder might be from yesterday's deadline. The tension in your jaw could be from words left unsaid. The tightness in your lower back might carry the weight of responsibilities you've been carrying. Progressive relaxation offers a way to listen to these stories and then, consciously, let them go.

Here's how to practice:

Find a comfortable position, either lying down or sitting with support. Take a few moments to settle and then:

Start With Your Feet

- Curl your toes tightly and press your feet downward.
- Hold this tension for five slow counts.
- Release completely, letting your feet become heavy.
- Notice the warmth or tingling that follows.

Move to Your Legs

- Tighten your calves, then your thighs.
- Make your legs rigid as boards.
- Hold, feeling the intensity build.
- Let go completely, feeling the muscles soften.

Work Through Your Core

- Tighten your belly, your back, your chest.
- Create tension across your torso.
- Hold briefly, then release with a deep exhale.
- Feel how your body sinks deeper into rest.

Finally, Your Arms and Face

- Make fists, tighten your arms.
- Scrunch your face, clench your jaw.
- Hold briefly.
- Release with a sigh.

End with a full-body scan, noticing the difference between how you feel now and when you started. This practice teaches your body the difference between tension and relaxation, building awareness of when you're holding stress and giving you the tools to release it.

Visualization: Your Mind's Natural Power

It means you've already started creating it if you can see it. Your mind paints pictures all day long—when you remember breakfast, plan your route to work, or imagine meeting a friend for coffee. This natural ability to create mental images makes visualization one of our most powerful tools for finding calm.

Think of visualization as creating a movie in your mind, but one where you can feel the temperature, smell the air, and hear every sound. Choose a place where peace lives for you:

Maybe it's a beach:

- Feel the warm sand between your toes.
- Listen to waves rolling in and out.
- Smell salt air mixing with sunscreen.

- Watch sunlight dancing on the water.
- Feel a gentle breeze on your skin.

Or perhaps a quiet forest:

- Notice dappled sunlight through leaves.
- Feel the soft earth beneath your feet.
- Listen to birds calling overhead.
- Smell pine needles and fresh earth.
- Touch the rough bark of ancient trees.

Make this place your anchor, keep it available whenever you need it. During a stressful meeting, remind yourself of the feeling of sand between your toes. Your body will respond to the soothing images you conjure as if they were real. These thoughts will release the tension, slow your breathing, and bring you back to the center. After being diagnosed with leukemia, I had to get my blood drawn a lot. I had been terrified of needles my whole life. To overcome the anxiety, I started a somatic practice of finding something pleasing to look at in the room. When I focused on it, I didn't focus on the item but on the feeling in my body.

Noticing how something is pleasing or relaxing to you, while also observing the changes in your body, is rooted in mindfulness and body awareness. This practice helps bridge the mind-body connection and enhances your ability to experience and sustain positive sensations. Here's an overview of how it works and its benefits:

What Is It?

Somatic noticing is a mindfulness-based practice where you intentionally focus on your body's sensations when you encounter something enjoyable or relaxing. This might include:

- The warmth of sunlight on your skin.

- The scent of a favorite candle.

- The sensation of deep breathing during a calming moment.

Instead of just thinking, "This feels good," you direct your attention to **how it feels good in your body**—the physical sensations associated with relaxation or pleasure.

How to Practice Somatic Noticing

1. **Identify a Relaxing or Pleasing Stimulus**:
   Choose something that brings you comfort or joy, like soft music, a warm beverage, or the feeling of lying down after a long day.

2. **Focus on Sensations**:
   Notice the physical sensations this experience evokes. For example:

   - Does your breathing slow down?

   - Do your shoulders relax?

   - Is there a feeling of warmth, lightness, or ease in certain parts of your body?

3. **Name the Changes**:
Mentally or verbally label what you notice. For example:

- "My chest feels warm."

- "My jaw is loosening."

- "I feel a tingling in my hands."

4. **Stay Present**:
Allow yourself to stay with these sensations without judgment or analysis. Simply observe them as they unfold or shift.

5. **Anchor the Experience**:
Acknowledge that this pleasant sensation is happening right now. This helps create a positive association and reinforces the connection between relaxation and your body.

Benefits of Somatic Noticing

- **Enhanced Self-Awareness**: You become more attuned to your body's signals, which can help you recognize both stress and calm states more clearly.

- **Improved Stress Regulation**: Regularly noticing and naming relaxing sensations can train your nervous system to return to a calm state more quickly after stress.

- **Increased Enjoyment**: Savoring positive moments deepens your ability to fully experience pleasure, contributing to overall well-being.

- **Stronger Mind-Body Connection**: By focusing on physical sensations, you reinforce the idea that your mind and body work together to create your experience.

An Example of Somatic Noticing

Imagine you're sitting outside on a cool, sunny day. You feel the warmth of the sun on your face.

1. Take a moment to notice how your muscles soften as the warmth spreads.

2. Observe that your breathing slows and deepens.

3. Mentally note, "I feel lighter. My shoulders are less tense."

4. Stay with this sensation, letting it anchor you in the present moment.

This practice helps you not only enjoy the experience but also trains your nervous system to recognize and amplify positive states. Over time, it can enhance resilience, mindfulness, and emotional balance.

Finding Joy in What Is

Gratitude helps remind us we are alive. It simplifies finding joy in daily things, like the gentle squeeze of a hand when words fail. When we notice these things, we remember that we're not just surviving our days, but collecting moments that make life worth living.

Simple Ways to Practice Gratitude

Create a Gratitude Ritual

May we cling to the ritual of remembering what is good and the good things that get us up and keep us moving when everything else feels heavy. Anchor your day with small, peaceful moments: coffee, commute, sleep.

Choose one of these moments to make your own:

- While your coffee brews, warm your kitchen with its aroma.

- During your commute, as the world slowly wakes around you.

- Before dinner when you are approaching the evening.

- Just before sleep, when tomorrow hasn't yet made its demands.

Use this time to notice three things that brought light to your day. Maybe it was how your child reached for your hand without being asked. Or how the trees along your street turned gold in the afternoon sun. Or the text from a friend that arrived just when you needed it most.

Share Your Appreciation

When was the last time you said thank you to someone? Or, the last time you called your best friend on a random Tuesday to tell them you think their presence in your life is a gift? We often hold appreciation without letting it reach the people who've earned it. We save our gratitude for big moments, holidays, and celebrations, forgetting that ordinary days also need this kind of magic. These acts of kindness deserve to be seen, named, and celebrated.

Start small:

- Send that text you've been meaning to send.

- Leave a note for someone who makes your workday better.

- Tell your partner one specific thing you appreciate about them.

- Thank the person who always makes your day smoother.

Simple words like "I noticed what you did" or "You made my day better" create ripples of connection. They remind us that we're all part of each other's stories and that the smallest gestures can be meaningful.

Practice Presence in Small Moments

There will be tough days when finding anything to be grateful for feels impossible. But if you keep practicing, you'll discover it becomes naturally easier to appreciate small moments and find that sense of peace you're looking for. Begin by noticing these kinds of small moments each day-it's a more in-depth try of the adage "stop and smell the flowers".

- Someone is saying your name with love.

- Fresh sheets are against your skin.

- Cold water when you're thirsty.

- Quiet moments before you fall asleep.

- Pets that love us without condition.

- Starting again after failure.

- Trees tops moving with the wind.

- Moments when someone sees you.

Each of these moments shows that even on the hardest days, life offers small gifts of grace. Gratitude is about focusing on what's still good—and often, that's more than we realize.

Chapter Eight

Social Connections and Support Systems

Having people you can count on is a powerful gift. It's friends who bake cookies with you, sit with you in the emergency room, or just listen when you need to talk. These connections matter. They create a safety net—someone bringing soup when you're sick, sharing a laugh when you're down, or simply showing up when you need them most.

We often talk about doing everything on our own, but the truth is we need each other. My family of origin created a need for complete self reliance. We call that "avoidant" attachment-a topic for another book[1]. It took a lot of work to create a life with social support for me. Some are lucky enough to learn this from our families growing up. Others find it later through friends who become family. Either

---

1. The Complete Guide To Attachment Styles: Learn to Navigate Anxious and Avoidant Patterns - How to Build Trust and Connection - Break Through Barriers to Vulnerability - Tools and Techniques https://www.amazon.com/dp/B0DS1L8VF8

way, these relationships aren't just nice to have - they're essential to how we handle life's trials.

The Science of Social Support

People need people, regardless of how independent we claim to be, how many walls we build, and how often we say we're fine on our own. This is a truth that is deeply embedded in our biology and woven into the very fabric of our nervous systems. When we connect with others, our bodies respond in measurable ways: stress hormones drop, heart rates steady, and muscles relax.

Think about how you feel when a friend sits with you during a difficult moment. Your breathing slows. Your shoulders drop away from your ears. Something in you recognizes: I'm not alone in this. This isn't just emotional comfort—it's your body's stress response system getting the message that it's safe to stand down.

Research by Szollosi and Newell (2020) shows us what we've always intuitively known: having people in our corner changes everything. When we know someone has our back, we handle challenges better. Problems feel more manageable. The world feels less overwhelming. Studies find that people with strong social connections generally sleep better, heal faster, and show more resilience in the face of stress.

Our brains actually work differently when we feel supported. That warm feeling you get when someone really listens to you? That's your brain releasing oxytocin, often called the bonding hormone. Do you feel a sense of relief after venting to a friend? That's your nervous system being regulated by social connection. Every supportive interaction creates pathways in our brains that make future connections easier, stronger, and more natural.

This is why isolating ourselves when we're struggling often backfires. Our systems are built for connection and designed to function best in the context of supportive relationships. Even introverts, who may need more alone time to recharge, still benefit deeply from having reliable social bonds. We're not meant to carry life's burdens alone—not just emotionally, but biologically.

Building Your Circle of Support

I am sure that at some point or another, you might have sat down and asked yourself this question: How do I find my people when it seems like everyone else already has their circles figured out? Sometimes scrolling through social media makes the world feel overwhelming yet lonely at the same time. You see photos of friends at brunches and birthday parties. It can make you wonder if you missed some secret instruction manual on how to build genuine connections with people.

The truth is that building real friendships takes time and patience. Not every attempt at connection will turn into a lasting relationship, and that's okay. The meaningful friendships that do develop are worth all the waiting, the awkward first conversations, and the times you had to push yourself to be brave.

Start Where You Are

Yes, where you are is a good enough place to start because that's where life is already happening. Your routines, your regular haunts, your daily rhythms—these aren't just habits, they're potential doorways to connection. The familiar faces you see but haven't really met yet, the silent nods of recognition that could become conversations, the shared moments waiting to unfold.

Look around at the spaces you already occupy:

- The coffee shop where you work remotely, where someone else might crave company too.

- The gym class where you share triumphant grins after surviving another tough workout.

- The online communities where you're already talking about things you love.

- The neighborhood where your evening walks might cross paths with others seeking quiet moments.

- The places where your passions naturally lead you, where kindred spirits gather.

These every day spaces hold more potential than we often realize. The person who orders the same complicated coffee drink as you might become a friend who gets your quirks. Your neighbor who walks their dog at the same time could become someone who checks on you when you're sick. Or, the colleague who laughs at your obscure references might become the friend who makes Mondays feel less mundane.

Connection doesn't always require grand gestures or completely new beginnings. Sometimes it's as simple as looking up from your laptop, making eye contact, offering a genuine smile, or commenting on the book someone's reading. These small moments of reaching out ripple outward, creating possibilities for deeper connections right where you already are.

Create Opportunities for Connection

Reaching is better than not reaching, and yes, sometimes reaching feels impossible, feels vulnerable, and feels like too much of a risk. Every meaningful connection in your life began because someone was brave enough to reach out first. The best friend who knows all your stories? Someone had to start that first conversation. The group that feels like family? Someone had to organize that first gathering.

Sometimes finding your people means becoming the person who creates the spaces where connections can happen:

- Start a book club in your apartment complex, where stories become bridges between neighbors.

- Organize a weekly coffee meetup for remote workers who understand the quiet loneliness of home offices.

- Join a volunteer group for a cause you care about, where shared values create natural bonds.

- Take a class that excites you. Where learning something new means learning about each other, too.

- Say yes to invitations, even when your couch calls louder than the party.

These activities are invitations to connection. Each one is a chance to meet someone who might become important in your story. Authentic connections often start small. A shared laugh over a common interest. A moment of vulnerability someone else recognizes. A simple "me too" that bridges the gap between strangers and friends.

There is so much magic in these small beginnings, in the courage it takes to show up, in the willingness to be the one who starts something new.

Learning to Communicate Well

Have you ever noticed how some people make you feel completely seen when they listen to you? How their whole body turns toward you, how their eyes stay with yours, how they seem to hear not just your words but the feelings behind them? This is what true communication looks like—not just an exchange of words, but a dance of presence and understanding.

Active Listening: More Than Just Hearing

When someone shares their story with you, they're offering more than just information—they're offering a piece of themselves. Active listening means receiving this gift with your full attention. It means putting down your phone, turning away from your screen, and bringing your whole self to the conversation. Simple gestures—a nod, a thoughtful "hmm," a gentle follow-up question—tell the other person: "I'm here with you. Your words matter to me."

The Silent Language of Bodies

Our bodies speak volumes before we say a word, carrying messages older than language itself. Watch two friends in deep conversation—how they mirror each other's postures without realizing it, how they create a bubble of shared space that feels almost visible. Notice how a mother instinctively opens her arms when her child is upset, how lovers naturally turn toward each other like flowers following the sun.

This wordless conversation happens in every interaction:

- A slight lean forward says "I'm interested in what you're sharing,"

- Open palms suggest, "I have nothing to hide, I'm here to connect,"

- Relaxed shoulders signal "I feel safe with you"

- Eye contact balanced with gentle breaks shows "I'm engaged but not overwhelming"

- A genuine smile that crinkles the eyes whispers "I'm truly happy to be here with you"

These movements are all natural expressions of authentic presence, so when we're fully engaged with someone, our bodies will naturally align with our attention. It's why we unconsciously match breathing patterns with people we're close to, why we find ourselves nodding along with someone's story before we've even processed their words.

The Gift of Constructive Feedback

Words have weight. Words can lift someone up or press them down. They can open doors or build walls. They can create bridges or dig trenches. When we give feedback, we join someone's story. We shape how they see themselves and their abilities.

Feedback should always come from a place of genuine care. It should highlight the spark in someone's presentation style before suggesting ways to improve their structure. It should celebrate their creativity while thoughtfully exploring how to enhance execution.

The most helpful feedback feels like a conversation between equals, not a judgment handed down. It opens with curiosity: "I noticed this approach you took—can you tell me more about your thinking here?" Sharing your perspective rather than prescribing solutions: "Here's what I observed, and here's what I wonder about." Inviting dialogue rather than demanding change.

Be patient and present; understand not just what someone is doing, but why they're doing it that way. Choose words that build confidence alongside competence. Because ultimately, good feedback it's about helping someone recognize and refine their own unique way of moving through the world.

Growing Your Emotional Intelligence

Understanding emotions—yours and others'—is like learning a new language. It speaks through quickened heartbeats and tense shoulders. It shows in subtle shifts of tone and minor changes in expression.

Start with yourself. Notice how anticipation flutters in your stomach before important meetings. Pay attention to how your voice changes when you feel defensive. Watch how your breathing shifts when someone touches a sensitive topic. This self-awareness develops through consistent practice.

In quiet moments:

- Notice your default emotional state upon waking.
- Track how your mood shifts throughout the day.
- Observe what situations consistently affect your energy.
- Pay attention to when you feel most like yourself.

In conversations:

- Feel how your body responds to different people.
- Notice which topics make you lean in or pull back.
- Watch how your thoughts change with your emotions.
- Listen for the feelings hiding behind your automatic responses.

In challenging situations:

- Recognize your first instinct when stressed.
- Observe how you handle unexpected changes.
- Notice what you do when feeling overwhelmed.
- Pay attention to your recovery patterns after difficulty.

When we focus on understanding our emotions well enough, rather than changing or controlling them, we naturally become better at understanding others, and of course, ourselves, too.

Navigating the Comparison Trap

We will be who we are at different points and junctures in our lives. We will be messy, we will be uncertain, we will be in progress and imperfect and still figuring things out. Some days we'll have it all together, and other days we'll wear mismatched socks and forget important meetings. Some years we'll soar, and others we'll barely keep our feet on the ground. This is what it means to be human, to be real, to be alive.

Yet we scroll through our phones, seeing only perfect moments, filtered lives, and carefully constructed narratives of constant success. Our messy reality meets their curated highlights, and something in us aches with the difference. We forget there's a person behind every polished post. Someone who wakes up wondering if they're enough. Or who sits with doubt? Someone who navigates the gap between how they seem and who they really are.

Your friend posting about their dream job might still get the Sunday night jitters. That couple sharing their perfect vacation photos argued about directions ten minutes before the sunset shot. Everyone crops their struggles out of the frame, leaving only the highlight reel for public viewing.

Understanding Your Comparison Patterns

Our tendency to compare ourselves to others has patterns, like waves that rise and fall throughout our days and seasons. Pay attention to when these waves hit hardest:

When We Feel Most Vulnerable:

- Scrolling through social media first thing in the morning, before we've even fully claimed the day as our own.

- During major life transitions, when everything feels uncertain and everyone else seems to have a map we never received.

- After receiving the good news that somehow still feels inadequate because someone else's news seems bigger, brighter.

- In professional settings where success seems clearly defined by titles and promotions, while our own path feels messier.

- At family gatherings where progress is measured in milestones—marriages, babies, houses, promotions—as if life moves in only one direction.

- Late at night, when loneliness amplifies every perceived lack.

- On birthdays and new years, when time itself seems to demand an accounting of our achievements.

These moments of comparison tell us something important—not about our worth, but about what we value deeply. They point to the dreams we haven't dared to voice, the paths we're afraid to take, the parts of ourselves waiting to be acknowledged. Each pang of comparison is really a messenger asking us to listen more closely to our own hearts.

Watch how these feelings shift and change:

- Notice which comparisons sting the most.

- Pay attention to when you feel most secure in your own path.

- Observe what triggers self-doubt and what builds confidence.

- Listen to the quiet voice beneath the comparison—what is it asking for?

Turning Comparison Into Connection

Each moment of comparison holds a gift—a window into our own deepest wishes. When someone's success stirs something in us, it often illuminates a dream waiting to be acknowledged. When we feel drawn to someone else's path, it might reveal the direction our own heart longs to explore. Our responses to others can serve as compasses, pointing us toward our truths.

Think of comparison as a messenger bringing news about your own desires. That pull you feel toward someone's creative work speaks to the artist in you. Your attention to others' travels reveals your own spirit of adventure. The way you light up listening to stories of someone's business success shows your entrepreneurial spirit. Your fascination with others' home spaces points to your own nesting instincts. The warmth you feel seeing close friendships reflects your readiness for deeper connections.

The practice becomes simple: notice which achievements catch your attention, explore the stories that arise in these moments, and listen for the wishes whispering beneath your awareness. Let each comparison become an invitation to self-discovery, an opportunity to understand yourself more deeply. This transforms comparison from a source of separation into a bridge—connecting you more deeply with your own path while appreciating the light others shine on it.

Chapter Nine

Empowerment Through Action

This chapter is about transforming your daily life into a resilience-building practice. True empowerment isn't a destination—it's the ongoing process of building unshakeable inner strength through your choices, relationships, and actions. Every connection you make, every goal you pursue, and every small promise you keep to yourself becomes another building block in your foundation of resilience.

The Importance of Social Relationships

Having friends and family members provides significant benefits. People with strong social connections can receive practical help, such as having someone bake cookies with them on weekends or accompany them to emergency rooms. They have people to contact when experiencing powerful emotions, whether positive or negative. These relationships provide emotional support through physical presence and reliable help.

Social connections create reliable support systems in our lives. This includes friends who provide meals during illness, family members who offer emotional support, and coworkers who perform small acts of kindness. Humans benefit from community and social bonds, sharing experiences, and supporting others.

While society often emphasizes independence, research shows that interpersonal connections enhance our resilience. Some individuals experience strong family relationships from childhood, while others develop meaningful friendships that become equally significant later in life.

Strong relationships don't just make life more enjoyable—they create a resilience network that helps you weather any storm. When you invest in meaningful connections, you're building social resilience that strengthens your capacity to handle challenges and bounce back from setbacks.

Research on Social Support

We know humans require social interaction, regardless of personal preferences for independence or solitude. Biological studies and research on nervous system function document this need. Social connections create measurable physical effects, including reduced stress hormones, stabilized heart rates, and decreased muscle tension.

When someone provides support during difficult situations, it creates physiological changes. These include slower breathing and reduced physical tension. The presence of support helps individuals process challenging situations more effectively.

Research by Szollosi and Newell (2020) demonstrates that social support improves various aspects of life. People handle difficulties more effectively when they have reliable support. We know humans require that individuals with strong social relationships experience improved sleep quality, faster illness recovery, and increased stress management ability.

Social support affects brain function. Listening to a supportive person triggers the release of oxytocin, a hormone associated with bonding. Discussing problems with others helps regulate the nervous system. Regular supportive interactions strengthen neural pathways related to social connection.

Self-imposed isolation during difficult periods often proves counterproductive. Research shows that social relationships benefit both physical and emotional health. This also applies to introverted individuals, though they may require more time between social interactions.

Building Connections in Your Everyday Life

Start by looking at your current environment and daily activities. You'll find many opportunities for connection in the places you regularly visit, whether physical or virtual. Remote workspaces, exercise classes, digital communities, neighborhood events, and interest-based groups all provide natural settings to meet others. These spaces are more than just backdrops to your routine; they're fertile ground for developing relationships.

Often, meaningful connections grow from the simplest interactions. A shared smile, eye contact, or a kind comment about a mutual interest can open the door to a deeper bond. Over time, colleagues who share your hobbies or neighbors you greet regularly can grow into trusted friends. These small gestures lay the foundation for relationships that offer support and companionship when you need them most.

Creating Opportunities for Social Interaction

Making meaningful connections often requires intentional effort. Every close relationship begins with someone taking the first step. This might mean organizing a book club in your neighborhood, setting up regular meetups for remote workers, or volunteering for a community project. You could also join an educational program or simply say "yes" to more social invitations.

These activities don't just fill your schedule—they create moments of shared experience where bonds can naturally form. Whether it's through discovering a shared interest or working toward a common goal, these connections often emerge in places where you choose to engage fully.

Communication as the Key to Connection

At the heart of any meaningful relationship is effective communication. Some people have a natural ability to make others feel heard through active listening, genuine eye contact, and an intuitive understanding of emotions. But anyone willing to invest in their interactions can practice and improve these skills.

Active Listening

Listening is more than hearing someone's words—it's about showing you care. When someone shares their thoughts or feelings, they're offering you their trust. Active listening means setting aside distractions, being fully present, and responding thoughtfully. Ask questions that show your curiosity and reflect on what they've shared.

Non-Verbal Communication

Body language speaks volumes, often louder than words. Leaning forward signals interest, while open hands suggest honesty. Relaxed shoulders convey comfort, and consistent eye contact shows engagement. A sincere smile or a warm expression can make someone feel understood before you even say a word.

By combining active listening with meaningful non-verbal cues, you create a space where others feel valued. These small but significant behaviors form the building blocks of connection, helping you foster relationships that are as authentic as they are lasting.

Focusing on these practices can transform routine encounters into meaningful moments, and over time, those moments become the relationships that enrich your life.

Providing Constructive Input

Communication affects others' self-perception and capabilities. Helpful input acknowledges positive aspects while suggesting improvements. This approach treats both parties equally and encourages discussion rather than issuing directives.

Effective feedback requires understanding others' perspectives and methods. Use language that builds confidence while suggesting improvements.

Understanding Emotions

Recognizing emotional patterns requires attention to physical and verbal cues. Begin with self-observation. Notice physical responses to situations, changes in vocal tone during discussions, and breathing patterns when addressing sensitive topics.

Practice emotional awareness:

During quiet periods:

- Identify morning emotional states

- Monitor emotional changes throughout days

- Identify situations affecting energy levels

- Recognize periods of emotional comfort

During social interactions:

- Monitor physical responses to different people

- Identify engaging and challenging topics

- Observe thought patterns during emotional states

- Recognize automatic emotional responses

During difficulties:

- Identify stress responses

- Monitor reactions to unexpected changes

- Recognize signs of emotional strain

- Observe recovery patterns

Understanding personal emotions improves comprehension of others' emotional experiences. Social media presents selective aspects of others' lives. These curated presentations often exclude common difficulties. Remember that individuals posting professional achievements still experience workplace anxiety. Couples sharing vacation photos encounter typical relationship challenges. Social media personalities experience common insecurities.

Common triggering situations:

- Morning social media viewing

- Life changes

- Others' achievements

- Professional environments

- Family events

These comparison triggers indicate personal values and aspirations. They often highlight unaddressed goals or desired changes. When this happens, try to focus in on your response to these triggers. Just sit and notice. Don't judge or admonish yourself for your feelings.

Understanding Personal Empowerment

Research shows that personal empowerment encompasses multiple psychological, social, and behavioral dimensions (Zimmerman, 2000). We understand that empowerment manifests through increased self-efficacy, the development of individual agency, and enhanced decision-making capabilities (Cattaneo & Chapman, 2010).

The following perspectives illustrate various ways individuals understand and experience empowerment in their daily lives:

Self-Care and Daily Habits: "Empowerment is making my bed every morning even when the world feels too heavy to face. It's choosing myself over and over again."

Boundary Setting: "When I finally learned to say no without adding an explanation."

Generational Connection: "The moment I realized my grandmother's hands look exactly like mine, and all her strength lives in my bones too."

Personal Growth: "Starting my garden after everyone said I kill every plant I touch. Now I grow my food."

Cultural Heritage: "Walking into rooms knowing my ancestors cleared the path for me to be here."

Parental Influence: "Teaching my daughter that her voice deserves to fill up space."

Individual Development: "Realizing that healing happens at my pace, and that pace is perfect."

Personal Agency: "The day I stopped waiting for permission to create the life I wanted."

Self-Acceptance: "Understanding that my sensitivity is actually my superpower."

Progress Recognition: "When I finally saw that every small step forward still counts as progress."

These perspectives align with established research on psychological empowerment. Rappaport's (1987) foundational work identifies three key components of empowerment: personal control, critical awareness, and participation. More recent studies by Peterson et al. (2014) demonstrate that personal empowerment often develops through small, daily actions and realizations similar to those described in these examples.

Research by Christens (2012) suggests that empowerment operates at multiple levels: individual, organizational, and community. The above perspectives primarily reflect individual-level empowerment, characterized by increased self-efficacy and personal agency. This aligns with Diener and Biswas-Diener's (2005) findings that psychological empowerment often manifests through improved self-perception and decision-making abilities.

These expressions of empowerment show each moment of choosing yourself, setting boundaries, or recognizing your progress represents your growing capacity to handle life's challenges with strength and grace.

Setting and Achieving Personal Goals

Our grandparents used to tell a bedtime story about a young girl who wanted to touch the moon. Every night, she would climb the tallest hill near her house, stretch her arms toward the sky, and try to grasp that glowing orb. Her parents told her it was impossible, that the moon was too far away, that some dreams were too big. But instead of giving up, she started building a ladder. One rung at a time, one day at a time. She gathered materials, learned about construction, and studied the stars. While she never touched the moon, she became an astronomer, an astronaut, and the first person from her village to go to space.

This story holds a truth about achieving our dreams—not in one giant leap, but in small, deliberate steps. Each rung of the ladder matters. Each skill we learn, each small victory we claim, and each moment we choose to keep going despite doubt or difficulty brings us closer to our goals.

The real power of goal-setting lies in transforming dreams into plans. When we say, "I want to write a book," we start with a single page. When we dream of running a marathon, we begin with a walk around the block. These aren't just first steps; they're declarations of possibility, promises we make to ourselves about who we're becoming.

Making Dreams Tangible

Tangible is a lovely word; lovely in the sense that it speaks to things we can hold, touch, and feel beneath our fingertips. Dreams dwell in clouds and moonlight, floating in the realms of "someday" and "maybe." But we live here, in the solid world of now. The magic happens when we bring those dreams down from their clouds, giving them shape, weight, and substance.

Want to open your bakery? Let flour dust your kitchen counters. Learn how yeast blooms in warm water. Master one perfect loaf of bread, then another. Dream of writing a novel? Let your pen meet the paper for ten minutes each morning. Watch your words accumulate like falling leaves. Do you see yourself running your own company? Take that first business class. Start that side project. Make that first sale. Let each small action be something you can touch, proving your dreams are more than just dreams.

The Architecture of Achievement

Every significant achievement starts with a clear vision, like constructing a building that will stand the test of time. This process begins with laying a solid foundation by making your goals specific and measurable. Instead of setting a vague goal to "get healthy," commit to cooking three weekly homemade meals. Rather than saying you want to "be more creative," dedicate thirty minutes daily to your art practice.

Once your foundation is secure, create a framework by breaking your larger goal into logical phases. Someone training for a marathon understands they must master running a single mile before tackling longer distances. A new business owner focuses on developing one solid idea, creating a thorough business plan, and securing their first customer before expanding.

Daily actions serve as the building blocks of your progress. These might include writing pages before starting your workday or taking photographs during lunch breaks to build your portfolio. Try listening to a podcast that encourages you in your pursuit. I enjoy practicing my French language during my morning commute. Each small action adds another brick to your structure, strengthening it and making it more stable.

Regular reflection will be your tool for quality control, allowing you to assess what you've built and make necessary adjustments. Acknowledge meaningful milestones,the first client who trusted your services, completing a run without stopping, or submitting your first story for publication. These moments of reflection help you understand which strategies are working and where your approach might need refinement.

Embracing Failure

Failure isn't a character flaw; it isn't something we need to be ashamed of; it isn't a mark against our worth or potential. Failure is simply information, a data point on the map of our progress. When we miss a day of practice, our bread refuses to rise, or our business proposal gets rejected. These moments offer us clarity about where we need to focus next.

Think of scientists in their labs, testing hypothesis after hypothesis. Each experiment that doesn't work brings them closer to understanding what will work. They call this process research, not failure. Artists create dozens of sketches before landing on their final composition. Writers draft and redraft until their words ring true. Entrepreneurs pivot their business models until they find what resonates with their market.

Every "no" carries the seeds of your next "yes." Every setback illuminates the path forward more clearly. These moments when you seem to fail are your best teachers. They show exactly where you need to improve your skills. They reveal where your plans need work. And they point to where you'll make your next breakthrough.

Promises To Yourself

When you make promises to yourself, you're essentially saying: I am worth the work. I am worth the effort I invest in myself to be better. Each promise kept becomes proof of this worth, a quiet affirmation that your words to yourself matter. Break your promises into small daily actions. Write for five minutes each morning. Save one dollar a day. Take a single step toward your dream. Each time you follow through, you build more trust in yourself.

Start with promises that feel tiny and simple. Before your coffee, drink one glass of water. Take a moment to read just one page at night. When morning comes, stretch for two minutes. Your kept promises show you can trust yourself. Success builds confidence. Meeting each small goal makes the next one easier.

You are working on building a relationship with yourself, and every time you say "I will" and follow through, you strengthen your belief in what's possible. Consistent, small daily actions bring your dreams closer, no matter how distant they seem.

The Power of Small Wins

Alice started her journey as a self-described pessimist. She couldn't see progress anywhere in her life. "Nothing ever works out," she would often say. She brushed off her daily achievements.

Then she created her "proof journal." Each day, she wrote one small win. She made her bed when depression made it feel impossible. She sent difficult emails one at a time. She cooked a meal instead of ordering takeout. When anxiety whispered to stay inside, she walked around the block.

Four weeks later, you would swear she was an entirely different person. She was JOY personified. Not because her life had dramatically changed but because she had learned to see it differently. "I used to wait for big moments to feel proud," she tells us. "Now I celebrate making coffee in the morning, attending meetings on time, remembering to water my plants. These tiny victories add up to something bigger—they add up to trust in myself."

Alice's story teaches us something vital about progress: it rarely announces itself with fanfare. Instead, it whispers through small moments of choice and action. The day you choose water instead of soda. In the morning, you wake up five minutes earlier. The moment you speak up in a meeting despite your racing heart. These victories might seem too small to celebrate, but they are powerful. Each proves that change is possible, that growth happens in inches, and that every small choice to show up for yourself matters.

Small wins are collectors of evidence, evidence that you can trust yourself, follow through, and handle more than you think. They build a case for your capability, one tiny victory at a time. They will be your anchors on days when progress feels impossible. You can look back at all these small wins and remember you've done hard things before. You can do them again.

Embracing Uncertainty

There are few things as sure as change itself. We see it in seasons shifting, in children growing, in cities growing, in hearts healing. Since around 500 BC, people have known this, quoting the Greek philosopher Heraclitus, who said, "Nothing is permanent except change."

Change moves through our lives like breath through our bodies—constant, necessary, life-giving. Yet often, we resist it, pressing our feet against its flow, trying to hold on to moments that were only meant to teach us, not keep us.

The most resilient people aren't those who never feel uncertain—they're the ones who have learned to trust their ability to adapt. Each challenge they face, each unexpected turn in their path, becomes evidence of their capacity to find their way through unfamiliar terrain. They've learned that security doesn't come from controlling circumstances, but knowing they can handle what comes their way.

You won't be someone who never feels afraid of change, but someone who builds trust in your ability to adapt and find your footing even when the ground shifts. Flexibility becomes your strength like a tree that bends in strong winds without breaking. Some of life's most beautiful moments are unplanned. A conversation with a stranger shifts your perspective. Or a detour leads to an unexpected adventure. A closed door points you to a better opportunity.

Look, joy or positivity doesn't come into your existence overnight; it's a series of choices and actions over time that build into something beautiful. Each small win you celebrate, each moment of uncertainty you navigate, and each promise you keep to yourself becomes another brushstroke in this masterpiece you're creating. Your life transforms not through grand gestures or dramatic changes but through these quiet moments of choosing—choosing to try again, staying open to possibility, and trusting your strength. This is how empowerment grows: one choice, one action, one moment at a time.

Chapter Ten

Creating Your Foundation for Long-Term Success

Genuine change isn't linear. It's a complex dance between progress and resistance, between old patterns trying to reassert themselves and new neural pathways forming with each small victory. Understanding this biological and psychological tug-of-war helps us approach change with both self-compassion and strategic intelligence.

The Architecture of Lasting Change

Deep behavioral change requires more than willpower – it demands a restructuring of our daily reality. While motivation fluctuates, carefully designed environments and routines can carry us through challenging periods. Think of your environment as a silent partner in change, one that can either subtly sabotage or consistently support your efforts.

Consider how your spaces tell stories about who you are and who you're becoming. A meditation cushion by your bedside doesn't just remind you to meditate – it speaks to an identity shift, a statement about the person you're growing into. Your environment should whisper encouragement in the language of visual cues and thoughtful arrangements.

Strategic environmental modifications might include:

- Creating a "morning sanctuary" where your first actions align with your intentions

- Designing workspaces that make healthy choices the path of least resistance

- Crafting evening spaces that naturally guide you toward rest and reflection

The Art of Habit Integration

Rather than forcing new habits into existence, we can weave them into the fabric of our existing routines. This process, often called habit stacking, works because it respects the brain's preference for familiar patterns while gradually expanding them.

But effective habit stacking goes beyond simple pairing. It's about understanding the emotional and energetic flows of your day. When are you naturally most receptive to new behaviors? Which existing habits carry positive emotional momentum that can lift new practices?

For example, instead of just adding meditation to your morning coffee routine, consider how the quiet anticipation of brewing coffee creates a natural space for mindfulness. Let the existing ritual enhance the new practice.

Navigating the Shadow Periods

Every meaningful change journey includes periods of doubt, resistance, and what can feel like regression. These shadow periods aren't failures – they're opportunities for deeper integration and understanding. During these times:

- Practice radical acceptance of where you are, while maintaining a gentle orientation toward growth

- Use "minimum viable actions"–tiny steps that keep you connected to your path without overwhelming your system

- View resistance as information rather than obstacle–what is it telling you about what needs attention or change?

Building Psychological Flexibility

True resilience isn't about becoming tougher – it's about becoming more adaptable. This involves developing a more nuanced relationship with our thoughts and experiences.

- Practice holding multiple perspectives simultaneously: "This is challenging AND I'm learning"

- Develop comfort with ambiguity and incomplete progress

- Cultivate curiosity about resistance and setbacks instead of immediate problem-solving

The Support Ecosystem

Sustainable change requires more than individual effort—it needs a nurturing ecosystem. This goes beyond having cheerleaders; it's about creating relationships that provide:

- Honest reflection without judgment
- Space for both struggle and celebration
- Shared wisdom and diverse perspectives
- Accountability that comes from connection rather than obligation

Daily Practices for Deep Integration

The most powerful practices are often the simplest, done consistently:

Morning:

- Begin with intentional presence before engagement with the world
- Set intentions that align with your deeper values, not just daily tasks

Throughout Day:

- Practice micro-moments of awareness
- Notice and celebrate small alignments with your intentions

Evening:

- Reflect on the day's experiences with curiosity rather than judgment

- Identify moments of growth, however subtle

- Create conditions for renewal rather than just rest

Remember, lasting change isn't about perfect execution—it's about persistent realignment. Each day offers countless opportunities to choose patterns that better serve your growth, to respond to challenges with increasing flexibility, and to build a life that reflects your deepest intentions.

Conclusion

A Nigerian proverb says, "In the moment of crisis, the wise build bridges, and the foolish build dams." Here you are, after all these pages, all these tools, and moments of learning to build differently.

You have learned effective methods for managing difficult thoughts after reading these chapters and working with these tools. Through practice, you understand how to create new possibilities when negative thinking occurs. When feeling the urge to withdraw, you've learned to seek support. Even small positive changes - a supportive thought, being kind to yourself, or asking for help - can lead to beneficial outcomes.

Methods for handling challenges will vary day by day. Sometimes you'll feel capable, ready to face significant doubts with confidence. Other moments might require focusing on getting through one difficult minute at a time. Personal coping strategies will develop during private moments of self-reflection, while additional skills will come from working with supportive people who understand your difficulties. Every step forward helps you progress. These new abilities transform you from someone who suppressed emotions into someone who processes feelings and thoughts effectively.

The next 30 days provide specific steps to improve how you interact with your thoughts. Daily work builds upon previous lessons to create positive, lasting changes. Success doesn't require perfection - focus instead on making steady progress through small, consistent improvements. The next section lays out a 30-Day Plan for you to follow, feel free to adjust as necessary and make it your own.

ou've discovered what it means to lay down planks of possibility when your thoughts try to construct walls. You've practiced reaching outward when everything in you wants to turn inward. You've learned that even the most minor bridge—a gentle thought, a moment of self-compassion, a hand extended for help—can lead you somewhere new.

Your bridges might look different on different days. Some days, they'll be grand structures of courage and hope, spanning wide rivers of doubt. On other days, they'll be simple rope bridges, strong enough to help you cross from one moment to the next. Some you'll build alone in quiet moments of self-trust, others you'll construct alongside people who understand your journey. Each one matters. Each one takes you further from the person who used to dam up their feelings, closer to someone who knows how to let emotions flow and thoughts transform.

Now, let's turn understanding into action. The next 30 days will guide you through practical steps to reshape your relationship with your thoughts. Each day builds on the last, creating a foundation for lasting change. Remember, this isn't about perfection—it's about progress and small steps that add to significant transformation.

30-Day Transformation Plan

Week One: Building Awareness

Day 1: Start with a thought audit. Throughout the day, keep a small notebook handy. Every time you catch a negative thought, write it down without judgment. Just observe and record. At the day's end, read through your notes. Notice any patterns.

Day 2: Focus on physical sensations that accompany negative thoughts. When a negative thought arises, pause and scan your body. Where do you feel tension? Document the connection between specific thoughts and physical responses.

Day 3: Teach yourself how to pause. Set three random alarms during your day. When they sound, stop and ask: "What am I thinking right now? Is this thought helping or limiting me?"

Day 4: Map your triggers. Notice what situations, times of day, or interactions spark negative thinking patterns. Record specific details: time of day, who was there, what happened just before, what thoughts followed.

Day 5: Begin morning pages—three pages of stream-of-consciousness writing first thing in the morning. Don't edit. Just let your thoughts flow onto paper. Notice what themes emerge when you give your mind free rein.

Day 6: Focus on language patterns. Notice words like "always," "never," "should," or "must." Each time you catch yourself using these absolute terms, write down what you were thinking and what prompted these thoughts.

Day 7: Weekly reflection. Look back through your week's observations. What patterns do you notice? Which times of day are the hardest? What situations consistently trigger negative thoughts? Write a reflection about what surprised you most about your thinking patterns.

Week Two: Developing New Responses

Day 8: Start reframing practice. Take three negative thoughts from your first week and write alternative perspectives for each. Focus on realistic rather than positive thinking.

Day 9: Create a morning ritual that grounds you. Maybe it's five minutes of deep breathing, a short walk, or mindful tea drinking. Choose something that feels natural and doable.

Day 10: Practice the "yet" technique. Add "yet" to the end of limiting thoughts. "I can't handle this" becomes "I can't handle this yet." Document how this small addition changes your perspective.

Day 11: Implement the pause-breathe-choose method. When negative thoughts arise, pause for three breaths before responding. Note how this gap affects your reactions.

Day 12: Start a victory journal. Write three things you handled well today, no matter how small. Build evidence of your capability.

Day 13: Practice thought-diffusion. When negative thoughts come, say "I'm having the thought that..." before them. Notice how this creates distance from the thought.

Day 14: Weekly reflection. Review your progress. What new patterns are you noticing? What techniques resonate most?

Week Three: Strengthening Your Foundation

Day 15: Begin body-based grounding. When thoughts spiral, focus on physical sensations—feet on the floor, hands on the desk, breath in body.

Day 16: Create a "worry window." Set aside 15 specific minutes for worrying. Outside that time, postpone worries to your next window.

Day 17: Practice self-compassion phrases. Write three go to phrases for tough moments. Use them when your inner critic gets loud.

Day 18: Start the "what's authentic right now" practice. When anxious about the future, list five things you know are true at this moment.

Day 19: Implement boundary setting. Choose one situation where you'll practice saying no or setting limits to protect your mental peace.

Day 20: Create an energy audit. Track what situations and people energize or drain you. Use this information to make conscious choices.

Day 21: Review and adjust. What's working best? What needs modification? Plan your final week based on your insights.

Week Four: Building Lasting Change

Day 22: Develop your personal mantra. Create a short, meaningful phrase that anchors you in difficult moments.

Day 23: Practice strategic disengagement. Choose one negative thinking trigger to limit or avoid today.

Day 24: Create a toolkit for tough days. List specific actions, people, and resources you can turn to when negative thoughts get loud.

Day 25: Implement the "future self" technique. Decide by asking what your wisest self would advise.

Day 26: Practice active appreciation. Counter each negative thought with a specific appreciation of something in your present moment.

Day 27: Build a success archive. Document past challenges you've overcome. Use these as evidence when doubt creeps in.

Day 28: Create morning and evening bookends. Develop simple rituals to start and end your day with intention.

Day 29: Practice strategic optimism. For each worry about the future, create one possible positive outcome.

Day 30: Integration and commitment. Review your month's journey. Choose three key practices to maintain from now on. Write a letter to yourself about continuing this path.

You are the builder, the creator, the one who can always choose to build another bridge, to reach toward another possibility, to connect with another moment of light. Keep building, reaching, and choosing bridges over dams.

References

Acosta, K. (2022, January 11). *What causes overthinking—and 6 ways to stop.* Forbes Health. https://www.forbes.com/health/mind/what-causes-overthinking-and-6-ways-to-stop/

Ashwell, S. (2019, January 8). *The five-minute technique I use to defeat negative self-talk.* Healthline. https://www.healthline.com/health/mental-health/self-talk-exercises

Barker, E. (2016, April 26). *10 ways to boost your emotional resilience, backed by research.* Time. https://time.com/4306492/boost-emotional-resilience/

Camins, S. (2021, November 8). *Four defusion exercises to challenge negative thinking.* Road to Growth Counseling. https://www.roadtogrowthcounseling.com/changing-negative-thinking/

Cattaneo, L. B., & Chapman, A. R. (2010). The process of empowerment: A model for use in research and practice. American Psychologist, 65(7), 646-659.

Cherry, K. (2023, May 3). *How resilience helps you cope with life's challenges.* Verywell Mind. https://www.verywellmind.com/what-is-resilience-2795059

Christens, B. D. (2012). Toward relational empowerment. American Journal of Community Psychology, 50(1-2), 114-128.

Chirumamilla, L. (2023, June 28). *5 thought exercises that can elevate your mental health.* Pacific Prime Thailand's Blog; Pacific Prime Thailand's Blog. https://www.pacificprime.co.th/blog/5-thought-exercises-that-can-elevate-your-mental-health/

Coaching, C. P. (2021, September 11). *How to break the negative thinking habit on your team.* Complete Performance Coaching. https://completeperformancecoaching.com/2021/09/11/how-to-break-the-negative-thinking-habit-on-your-team/

Cognitive defusion techniques and exercises. (n.d.). Cognitive Behavioral Therapy Los Angeles. https://cogbtherapy.com/cbt-blog/cognitive-defusion-techniques-and-exercises

Diener, E., & Biswas-Diener, R. (2005). Psychological empowerment and subjective well-being. Psychological Empowerment: Research and Applications, 125-140.

Empathy: Better with boundaries. (2023, October 24). Heidi Goehmann. https://heidigoehmann.com/articles/empathy-better-with-boundaries

Harvard Health Online Learning. (n.d.). *Positive psychology.* Retrieved January 4, 2025, from https://www.harvardhealthonlinelearning.com/courses/positive-psychology-2?utm_source=pll-portal&utm_medium=referral&utm_campaign=positive-psychology

Hexpoor, M. (n.d.). *Six ways for empaths to set healthy boundaries.* LinkedIn. https://www.linkedin.com/pulse/6-ways-empaths-set-healthy-boundaries-minou-hexspoor-pcc-eli-mp/

How to stop overthinking in a relationship five tips and signs. (2023, July 17). Anchor Light Therapy Collective. https://anchorlighttherapy.com/overthinking-in-a-relationship/

Jones, H. (2023, October 2). *Ten exercises that help you stop overthinking.* Verywell Health. https://www.verywellhealth.com/how-to-stop-overthinking-7570368

Mansueto G, Cavallo C, Palmieri S, Ruggiero GM, Sassaroli S, Caselli G. Adverse childhood experiences and repetitive negative thinking in adulthood: A systematic review. Clin Psychol Psychother. 2021 May;28(3):557-568. doi: 10.1002/cpp.2590. Epub 2021 Apr 16. PMID: 33861493.

Michaels, C. (2015, December 15). *8 writing exercises to fight negative thinking.* Small Business Bonfire. https://smallbusinessbonfire.com/fight-negative-thinking/

Monarth, H. (2024, April 5). *Three brain exercises to neutralize negative thinking and stop ruminating.* Forbes. https://www.forbes.com/sites/harrisonmonarth/2024/04/05/brain-exercises-to-stop-ruminating/

Neidich, H. (2021, January 2). *How to combat negative thinking: Resources, information, and exercises.* Haley Neidich. https://www.haleyneidich.com/how-to-combat-negative-thinking-resources-information-and-exercises/

Pedersen, T. (2018, October 4). *Four thought exercises to try to improve mental health.* Psych Central. https://psychcentral.com/blog/thought-watching-exercises-to-increase-awareness-reduce-anxiety

Peterson, N. A., et al. (2014). Measuring the intrapersonal component of psychological empowerment: Confirmatory factor analysis of the sociopolitical control scale. American Journal of Community Psychology, 53(3-4), 347-356.

Rappaport, J. (1987). Terms of empowerment/exemplars of prevention: Toward a theory for community psychology. American Journal of Community Psychology, 15(2), 121-148.

Scott, E. (2020, April 28). *Why emotional resilience is a trait you can develop*. Verywell Mind. https://www.verywellmind.com/emotional-resilience-is-a-trait-you-can-develop-3145235

Supporting and developing resilience in social work. (n.d.). Supporting and Developing Resilience in Social Work. https://www.open.edu/openlearn/health-sports-psychology/supporting-and-developing-resilience-social-work/content-section-1

Think your way out of negativity: 6 thought exercises that can save your mental health. (2024). CNET. https://www.cnet.com/health/mental/think-your-way-out-of-negativity-6-thought-exercises-that-can-save-your-mental-health/

Thomas, J. (2018, May 6). *Twelve reasons for developing greater emotional resilience.* Betterhelp; BetterHelp. https://www.betterhelp.com/advice/resilience/12-reasons-for-developing-greater-emotional-resilience/

Tugade, M. M., & Fredrickson, B. L. (2004). Resilient individuals use positive emotions to bounce back from negative emotional experiences. *Journal of Personality and Social Psychology, 86*(2), 320–333. https://doi.org/10.1037/0022-3514.86.2.320

Verma, P. (2019, January 6). *Destroy negativity from your mind with this simple exercise.* Medium. https://medium.com/the-mission/a-practical-hack-to-combat-negative-thoughts-in-2-minutes-or-less-cc3d1bddb3af

Wright, K. W. (2023, June 14). *15 ways to cultivate emotional resilience.* Day One | Your Journal for Life.

Zimmerman, M. A. (2000). Empowerment theory: Psychological, organizational, and community levels of analysis. Handbook of Community Psychology, 43-63.

www.ingramcontent.com/pod-product-compliance
Lightning Source LLC
LaVergne TN
LVHW092010090526
838202LV00002B/80